The growth
of Leicester

The text of a series of talks on the history of Leicester
arranged by the Department of Adult Education
of the University of Leicester and
broadcast by B.B.C. Radio Leicester in 1969

Edited by A. E. Brown

The growth of Leicester

Leicester University Press   1970

First published in 1970 by Leicester University Press

Distributed in North America by
Humanities Press Inc., New York

Copyright © Leicester University Press 1970

Designed by Arthur Lockwood

Set in Monotype Perpetua

Printed in Great Britain by
Western Printing Services Ltd, Bristol

ISBN 0 7185 1100 X

Contents

List of maps

Preface

The talks printed in this book formed a series arranged by the Department of Adult Education of the University of Leicester and broadcast on B.B.C. Radio Leicester during the months of February, March and April 1969. The aim was to offer a popular introduction to the history of Leicester with an emphasis on the visual evidence. Clearly with a series of short talks such as this it has not been possible to provide a fully comprehensive account, and contributors were therefore asked to select aspects of the development of the city which seemed to them significant in their particular specialist periods. After the conclusion of the series there was a demand for a printed version and the talks have therefore been reproduced substantially as they were given. The opportunity has also been taken to include the maps and reading lists supplied in the teaching notes which accompanied the original broadcasts.

The Editor is grateful to the following for permission to reproduce maps: to the City of Leicester Publicity Department for Map 2, reproduced from the pamphlet *Leicester Castle* by Dr Levi Fox, and for Map 6, drawn by H. Collinson and taken from the first (1948) edition of *History in Leicester* by C. D. B. Ellis; to Edgar Backus for Map 3, reproduced from *Medieval Leicester* by C. J. Billson; to the City of Leicester Museums for Map 4 and for the cover illustration; and to the Board of Leicester University Press for Map 5, reproduced from *Radical Leicester* by A. Temple Patterson. Map 1 was drawn by A. D. McWhirr and is reproduced with his permission, with acknowledgments to the City of Leicester Museums. Maps 7 and 8 are the work of D. V. Noble. The quotation on p. 15 is taken from the book *Roman Silchester* by G. C. Boon, with the permission of B.P.C. Publishing Ltd.

The Editor would like in particular to thank Professor J. Simmons of the University of Leicester for his considerable help in the initial organization of the series of broadcasts.

A. E. Brown

1

Roman Leicester

Leicester is justly proud of its Roman remains and has more to show of its Roman past than most large towns in Britain which were founded in that period. The Jewry Wall is in fact one of the largest standing fragments of a Roman civilian building in the country. But it is possible that there was a settlement of some kind on the site of Leicester before the Roman invasion. During the first century B.C. the south-east and parts of the east of England were settled by a warlike people from the Continent called the Belgae. The evidence for this comes partly from the pages of Julius Caesar, but also from a study of the distribution and development of the coins issued by their rulers and from the characteristic pottery which the people used. A distinctive group of coins shows that a group of Belgae had reached the east Midlands in the first century B.C., presumably establishing a political supremacy over the people already living there, and forming the tribal unit of the Coritani, which is known to have occupied the area now taken up by Leicestershire, Rutland, Lincolnshire, Nottinghamshire and perhaps Derbyshire in the pre-Roman period. Pottery of Belgic type belonging to the latter part of the first century B.C. has been found at Leicester and it seems likely that these people began the first settlement here some half a century or so before the Romans came.

The Roman army landed in A.D. 43 and quickly overran south-east England, establishing a defended frontier zone from Devon to the Humber to protect the newly conquered province. An important road, the Fosse Way, acted as a means of communication along this frontier area, with forts in front of it, along it and behind it, all linked together by roads. Leicester was one of these forts. It lies on the Fosse Way, the Gartree Road connected it with Colchester, which might have been an important military base at this early period, and another road, recently identified as running across Kirby Muxloe golf course, joined it to another fort at Mancetter near Nuneaton. A few traces of this early military phase have been found. In the Jewry Wall Museum you can see a tinned bronze plate which once formed part of the belt of a legionary soldier's uniform, together with a couple of other pieces of bronze work of a military character. In 1967 a short length of Roman defensive ditch was found to the west of the railway line which crosses the main road at West Bridge, but it is not yet certain what kind of military establishment this belonged to.

Leicester was probably a military station for 30 years or so, until the Romans withdrew their garrisons from the Midlands for fresh campaigns in the North. In that time a civilian settlement had in all probability grown up outside the defences of the fort, as seems to have happened elsewhere in Britain, consisting of traders and others attracted by the presence of a large body of regularly paid troops at a place with good connections by road with other parts of the Roman province.

When the army advanced northwards the territory of the Coritani was freed from direct military control, and the Romans had to develop a system of civilian administration for it. What they did was to make use of the old pre-Roman tribal organization of the region, and to adapt it to new requirements. The Coritani were given a tribal council consisting of the wealthier and more influential members of the local aristocracy. These councillors were known as decurions. Each year the decurions elected four of their number to form the executive government of the tribal area, acting under the general supervision of the governor of the whole province of Britain and of the chief financial officer. Thus the Coritani were ruled by the nobility who were their natural and familiar leaders, a sensible enough idea.

The tribal units into which much of Britain was divided each had a capital town from which local administration was conducted and Leicester was chosen to be the centre of government for the Coritani. This is known from the name of the place itself, which one of our sources gives as Ratae Coritanorum, that is Ratae of the Coritani, the chief town of the tribe. As such it had to be suitably equipped, and it required the well-laid-out streets and public buildings appropriate to an important town. The Roman government was very anxious that new subjects should adopt the outward trappings of Roman civilization and the central authorities no doubt played a part in the development of towns like Leicester.

Accordingly, Ratae was provided with a grid of straight streets meeting each other at right angles and dividing the town up into islands or 'insulae'. What is known of the street plan is shown on Map 1 (page 13), where the insulae are also numbered. You can also see how some of the existing streets of the town appear to follow approximately the lines of Roman predecessors. The main street of Leicester would have been the continuation of the Fosse Way through the town, perhaps represented today by the line of Silver Street, Guildhall Lane and Thornton Lane.

The most important public building in Roman Leicester was undoubtedly the forum and basilica, the centre of the administrative life of the Coritani. This has been located by excavation to the east of the Jewry Wall site, occupying a whole 'insula'. The map gives an indication of how it lay in relation to the modern street system. Not very much is known about the details of this building, but presumably it resembled such places elsewhere. The forum consisted of an open rectangular courtyard which served as a market-place and on three sides of this were rows of shops and offices, separated by roofed colonnades from the courtyard and from the streets running around the outside. The basilica occupied the fourth side of the rectangular area and by analogy with other towns would have consisted of a large aisled hall, with at the back a council chamber and offices for the use of the tribal government. One would normally have

Map 1   Roman Leicester

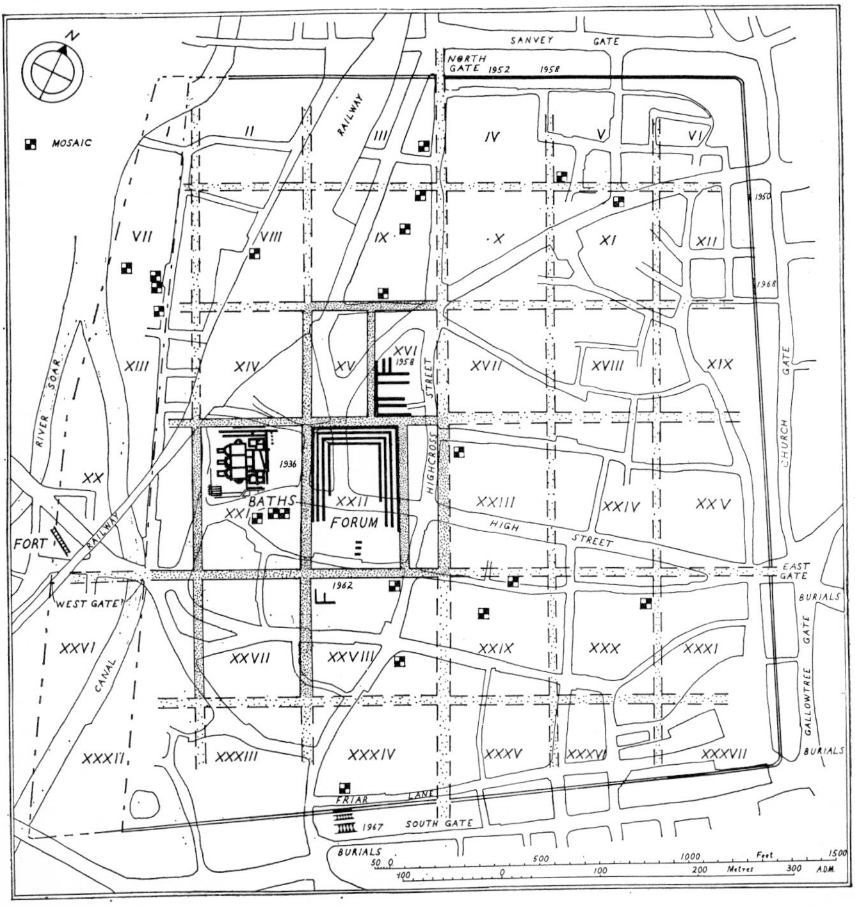

expected this large and important building, the ancient equivalent of a city or county hall, to have been built in a monumental style and to have been embellished with statues and decorative stonework. What has survived are some of the columns of the forum colonnade, which have been found in commercial excavations in the area over the last 100 years or so. Some fragments can be seen in St Nicholas' churchyard while others from the eastern side of the forum have been re-erected in front of the Jewry Wall Museum, together with a portion of the stone gutter which ran in front of the colonnade.

A second important building was the public baths, the remains of which are now laid out in front of the Jewry Wall Museum. Buildings of this sort were a regular feature of substantial towns in the Roman provinces and served a social need in addition to their cleansing function. They were places where one could relax, meet friends and discuss business, or merely gossip or gamble. The method of bathing was that of the present-day Turkish bath, which is derived from the Roman system. In a large establishment the bather entered a colonnaded courtyard or a large hall where exercises could be carried out. From the undressing room, he went through a series of rooms with progressively higher temperatures where perspiration would be induced. After a spell in the hottest room, he returned through the rooms in reverse order to the cold room, where he could have a shower or a cold plunge bath. The floors of the heated rooms were supported by pillars, and hot air generated by a furnace circulated underneath. The Jewry Wall itself represents the western wall of what was probably a covered exercise hall, and ran for the full width of the bath building from Welles Street in the north to St Nicholas Circle in the south. The side which now faces St Nicholas' church was intended to provide a dignified and impressive entrance to the bath suite to the west, and had four blank arches in it, the central pair of which are pierced by arched entrances leading to the baths, with a niche between to hold a statue. What remains today is a battered fragment, and in its original state the wall would have been adorned with ornamental stonework and coloured plaster. As the map shows, the rooms of the bathing establishment proper lay to the west of the Jewry Wall, and consisted of a symmetrically arranged series of rooms with furnaces at the extreme west of the site, now covered by the Jewry Wall Museum.

Work on the public baths began in the second quarter of the second century A.D., after earlier buildings on the site had been cleared away. The main framework of the building was soon put up, but a pause of some years seems to have followed before the whole scheme was completed. Once finished, the baths remained in use for some 250 years, to the end of the Roman period.

In their prime they must have been the scene of busy activity. In a

famous passage the philosopher Seneca, writing in the first century A.D., describes what it was like to live near a public baths.

Imagine all kinds of uproar, fit to make you hate your ears. The hearties are put through their paces, throw their hands about laden with leaden weights, and when they exert themselves, or pretend to, I hear their grunts and their whistling, raucous breathing. If the umpire of a ball-game makes an appearance, and starts to count the tosses, I'm done for. The picture is not complete without some quarrelsome fellow, a thief caught red-handed, or the man who loves the sound of his own voice in the bath – not to mention those who jump in with a tremendous splash. Besides those whose voices are good, think of the strident call of the barber, continually advertising his presence, never silent except when he plucks someone's arm-pits and forces his customer to cry out on his own behalf; or the assorted cries of the pastry-cook, the sausage-seller, the confectioner, and all the hawkers of refreshments selling their wares each in his own distinctive sing-song.

The Jewry Wall must have heard sounds much like this. Appropriately enough, among the objects found when the site was excavated were tweezers and other toilet implements, a bone comb, and some bone counters which could have been used in some kind of game.

The water-supply arrangements for the baths are not fully understood at present. A series of foundations added to the south-west corner of the site in the later second century might have carried a water tank. It has also been suggested that the Raw Dykes, a linear earthwork which formerly ran up to the city from the south, had been intended to act as an aqueduct but that owing to faulty levelling this arrangement had to be given up. But the Romans were skilled engineers and unlikely to make an elementary mistake like this, and recently it has been suggested that the Raw Dykes might have been a canal. The single surviving stretch of the Raw Dykes is in the care of Leicester Museum and can be seen to the west of Aylestone Road, near the power station.

Several of the tribal capitals in Britain had amphitheatres, at which the local councillors could provide shows and entertainments, such as bear-baiting, wrestling, cock-fighting and so on. No amphitheatre has been found at Leicester, but it might have had one nevertheless. A piece of pottery, pierced for suspension, has been found, with the inscription "Verecunda the actress and Lucius the gladiator" scratched upon it. And a glass cup found in Bath Lane in 1874 has the moulded figures of gladiators on it, with their names running around the top, just below the lip. It looks like a souvenir commemorating a popular team of gladiators which had toured the western provinces of the Empire.

Leicester was an important road centre and must have been a busy enough place. The tribal council would have had to maintain there a posting station for the use of travellers on official business, where they could stop for a night and obtain fresh horses. Although this building has not been identified we know it existed, because Leicester is one of the places mentioned in the Antonine Itinerary, a road book put together for official travellers in the early third century and listing routes and posting stations throughout the Empire.

Of the Roman roads radiating from Leicester, the Fosse Way at least had been fitted out with milestones. A fine example comes from Thurmaston and can be seen in the Jewry Wall Museum. It is of particular interest because it has the name of Leicester on it – it says that it is 2 miles from Ratae. Another milestone was found at Six Hills. The Thurmaston milestone has an inscription dating it to the reign of Hadrian, and perhaps the Fosse Way was extensively repaired and improved then. If it was, then we can be sure that the Coritani had to bear their share of the cost.

As a market centre Leicester seems to have flourished. It is quite possible that at some stage it was promoted in status and given a charter. In the later second century a second market hall was built, in Insula 16 to the north of the forum and basilica, which it seems to have resembled in general design. On market days these places would have had some resemblance to the Leicester market of today. In the Jewry Wall Museum can be seen some of the things which were sold – the famous red gloss samian ware imported in vast quantities from Gaul, coarse earthenware from local kilns like those at Earl Shilton and Desford or large manufacturing centres such as that near Peterborough, large pottery containers or amphorae which had held imported olive oil and wine, brooches and beads of all kinds, bronze objects and ironmongery. One of the shops in the forum of the tribal capital at Caerwent, in South Wales, seems to have been an oyster bar, to judge from the quantities of shells found in it. Oysters were popular in Roman Britain and plenty of shells come from Roman levels in Leicester; perhaps there was a similar establishment here. A modern equivalent would be a fish and chip shop. Buildings which may have been shops have been located elsewhere in Leicester – in Insula 15 for example, opposite the market hall. Shops in Roman towns were normally long buildings with a narrow street frontage. Small-scale manufacturing could be carried on at the back and goods laid out for display at the front.

The map shows the places at which mosaic pavements have been found. These would have belonged to the houses of the more well-to-do inhabitants, tribal councillors for example. One pavement can still be seen in its original position in Blackfriars because when the Great Central Railway was built over western Leicester at the end of the last century, a clause in the Act compelled the company to take steps to preserve it. Others have been removed to the Jewry Wall Museum. A house of some pretensions was excavated north of Blue Boar Lane in Insula 16 in 1958.

It consisted of a range of rooms fronted by a corridor and surrounding a courtyard. The walls had been decorated with wall paintings of high quality, with designs in excellent classical style in many colours. Considerable areas of this plaster have been reconstructed and can be seen at the Jewry Wall Museum, a very remarkable find. The house had been built in the earlier second century, but after a substantial decline in its fortunes was demolished to make way for the new market hall.

At some time in the late second or early third century Ratae was given stone walls. Their line is known on the north, south and east sides but what happened on the west is not certain. Excavation has shown that the wall was about 9 feet wide at the foundations, and had an earth backing behind it and a defensive ditch in front. The construction of the walls was an important event in Leicester's history since they fixed the outline of the town for many centuries to come. Nothing of this wall remains because its good building stone has been robbed away, but its general line can be seen along the north, where there is a marked slope downwards into Sanvey Gate from the interior of the town. A similar phenomenon can be seen in Churchgate, just to the north of its junction with Butt Close Lane.

In the fourth century Britain was under attack by enemies from Scotland and Ireland and by raiders from the continent. But archaeology gives no hint of any decline in the prosperity of Leicester. We know that the owners of the better-class houses could afford to have mosaic floors laid at this time, and alterations were made to the forum building, which might suggest a continuation of administrative vigour. This prosperity owed something at least to the continued efficiency of the town's defences; the town ditch was re-cut in the late Roman period and it is possible that the walls were improved, as elsewhere in Britain, by the addition of bastions to carry heavy catapults, the artillery of those days. Some hints about the arrangements made for the defence of Leicester and its surrounding area are offered by the presence in the Jewry Wall Museum of bronze fittings which are thought to belong to the uniforms worn by Germanic mercenary troops brought to Britain in the late fourth century by the Roman government to assist in warding off attacks from outside. The presence of barbarian troops at the turn of the fourth and fifth centuries may be the explanation for the existence just outside Leicester of the early Anglo-Saxon cemetery at Thurmaston and also the finding of another early Anglo-Saxon burial in Churchgate.

This force no doubt remained when in the early fifth century the main bulk of the imperial forces in Britain was withdrawn for service on the Continent. The tribal governments of Britain now had to fend for themselves, but there is no reason to suppose that a romanized town life in Leicester did not go on well into the century. It is an unfortunate fact that the later levels of the Roman town have been much disturbed by activity in the medieval and modern periods and therefore archaeology has as yet been unable to say much about the changing fortunes of the town in the sub-Roman period, or to fill out the meagre historical records of Saxon Leicester. But continuity there must have been. The walls survived and apparently the lines of some of the streets. The Jewry Wall may owe its remarkable survival to its incorporation in an early Saxon church. But for some reason the Roman name of the place did not survive; the Anglo-Saxons preferred to give the town a fresh name and not to adopt the old one. So it is Leicester, and not Ratchester.

Suggested reading

F. Haverfield, 'Roman Leicester', *Archaeological Journal*, LXXV, 1918.

M. Hebditch, 'Roman Leicester' in C. D. B. Ellis, *History in Leicester*, City of Leicester Publicity Department, 2nd edition 1969.

K. M. Kenyon, *Excavations at the Jewry Wall Site, Leicester*, 1948.

J. E. Mellor, 'Excavations in Leicester 1965–68', *Transactions of the Leicestershire Archaeological and Historical Society*, XLIV, 1968–9, 1–10.

Reviews of the Jewry Wall excavation report in *Journal of Roman Studies*, XXXIX, 1949, 142–5.

Note in *Journal of Roman Studies*, XLIX, 1959, 113–15 (excavations in Blue Boar Lane by J. S. Wacher).

The Jewry Wall, Leicester; Roman Mosaic Floors (pamphlets obtainable at the Jewry Wall Museum, Leicester).

2

Leicester Castle

The popular theory that Leicester Castle had its origin in Anglo-Saxon times and that it was built by Ethelfleda, lady of the Mercians, should no longer be taken seriously. On the contrary, it is to the years immediately following the Norman Conquest that the erection of a castle at Leicester must be attributed. The need for holding down a recently-subjected and resentful population led William the Conqueror to pursue a systematic policy of fortification, establishing castles in the larger towns and along the most important lines of communication. Some of these castles are mentioned in Domesday Book, in charters of the period or in contemporary chronicles, but others escaped mention altogether. This applies to Leicester Castle, the erection of which most probably took place in 1068, when in the course of a campaign which only lasted a month or two, William also erected castles at Warwick, Nottingham, York, Lincoln, Huntingdon and Cambridge, and probably at Stamford.

The site chosen for the castle at Leicester lay at the south-western angle of the town, upon the right bank of the River Soar – a position which suggests an invader anxious at once both to dominate the town and to preserve easy communication with the surrounding country. In its original form the castle consisted of an earthen mound (1)* surrounded by a ditch, with a wooden palisade on top and with a bailey or court below, surrounded by its own ditch, rampart and stockade. This was the typical pattern of the majority of early Norman castles in England. Any idea of the existence of a stone keep or other stone buildings at Leicester Castle at this period is completely erroneous. As it stands at present, the earth mound is about 30 feet high, but it was considerably higher until it was reduced and levelled for a bowling green just over a century ago.

The Conqueror entrusted Leicester to Hugh de Grentmesnil, who in reward for his services received extensive estates in Leicestershire, Warwickshire and other Midland counties. The castle thus became the residence of a Norman lord and the headquarters of a feudal 'honor', a

*The numbers in brackets refer to the parts of Leicester Castle as indicated on Map 2 (page 21).

term applied to a group of estates such as these which came under a single administration. His son, Ivo de Grentmesnil, who succeeded him, joined a rebellion against Henry I in 1101 and it seems clear that the castle was either destroyed or damaged at this time. Ivo later went on a crusade to reinstate himself but died whilst on it and his lands were granted to Robert de Beaumont, Count of Meulan. It is to this Robert, who later became the first earl of Leicester, that the rebuilding of the castle, as well as the church of St Mary-by-the-Castle (de Castro), is generally attributed. The surviving fragments of this early Norman church, incorporated in the subsequent rebuilding which took place about 1150, make it clear that it was a building of appreciable size and beauty (2); but in the absence of evidence, any statement regarding the nature of the rebuilding of the castle undertaken by Robert de Beaumont must be entirely conjectural.

Robert, called 'le Bossu', succeeded his father in 1118. Founder of Leicester Abbey, he also probably built the stone hall, the principal surviving part of the castle (3). Of late Norman style, the architecture of the hall at Leicester is somewhat earlier than that of Oakham, which it so much resembles, the latter being built about 1190. In both cases the hall consists of a nave and aisles at ground level, divided by pillars and pre-serving the primitive idea of an aisled hall. Robert 'le Bossu' died in 1168 and five years later his son Robert Blanchmains joined the rebellion of Henry, the king's son. While he was on a visit to Normandy, Robert's estates were confiscated and Leicester taken by royal forces and burnt. The castle itself held out but was surrendered the following year. In retaliation the king ordered the demolition of the castle's defences and of the town wall. Subsequently Robert was pardoned and most of his lands and castles were restored to him.

On the death of Robert Blanchmains in 1204 the castle passed to Amicia, one of the two co-heiresses who assumed the title of Countess of Leicester. After long drawn-out negotiations her son, Simon de Montfort, gained possession of all the estates of the honor of Leicester but on his death at Evesham in 1265 they were forfeited to the Crown and granted to the king's son, Edmund Crouchback. Edmund and his successors were earls of Lancaster and Derby as well as of Leicester and held a vast conglomeration of castles and manors scattered all over the country. Each castle, though administered as a separate unit, fitted into the larger territorial grouping and system of administration later known as the Duchy of Lancaster. On Edmund's death in 1296 the castle and estates were inherited by his son, Thomas of Lancaster, who was executed in 1324, then by Earl Henry who died in 1345, and Duke Henry who died in 1361, subsequently passing to John of Gaunt who made Leicester Castle one of his favourite residences until his death there in 1399.

Map 2   Leicester Castle

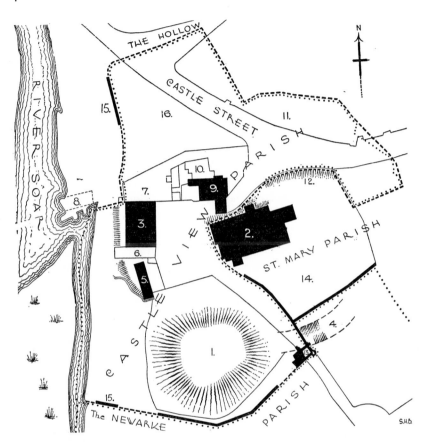

—— Modern boundaries, streets, etc.
----- Conjectural boundary of castle enclosure in early 15th century
━━ Existing remains of medieval boundary walls
...... Boundary of Castle View civil parish

1   Castle Mound
2   St Mary de Castro church
3   Castle Hall
4   Section of Norman ditch, excavated in 1939
5   John of Gaunt's cellar
6   Site of kitchen block, etc.
7   Site of Great Chamber
8   Site of Castle Mill (N.B. river course now altered)
9   Castle House and Gateway
10 House c. 1800 built over old cellar
11 Possible site of barbican
12 Bank (St Mary's Bank?)
13 Turret Gateway
14 Churchyard
15 Walls exposed in Castle Gardens
16 Site of original castle gardens

It is during the fourteenth century, the most splendid period in the castle's history, that an account of the buildings and activities which took place there first becomes possible. By now the residential aspect of the castle predominated over considerations of defence and more reliance was placed on the gateway (9), hard by St Mary's church, which commanded the castle enclosure, and on the wall around the bailey, portions of which can be seen to this day (15).

Within the enclosure the main buildings of the castle were built around a square court. At the far side running roughly parallel to the river stood the hall, an oblong building with sandstone walls $4\frac{1}{4}$ feet thick consisting of a nave and aisles of six bays, supported by arcades of timber. The hall formed the communal living room and dormitory for the majority of the castle residents. A large bay window provided light near the upper end where the dais and lord's table would be, and there were several smaller windows and possibly a fireplace or open hearth. From behind the dais stairs led to the great chamber (7) which afforded privacy for the lord and his family and guests and was also the nucleus of a suite of other private apartments.

Forming part of these domestic buildings was a private chapel for the use of the lord and his household. This would have been built because St Mary's church, although serving as a chapel in the early days of the castle, was apparently from the beginning a parish church as well. The receiver's accounts for 1313–14 contain an annual fee paid to the chaplain celebrating divine service in the castle chapel, while the accounts under John of Gaunt record payments to various chaplains and the duke's confessor, who presumably travelled with the household from place to place, as did also the chapel ornaments. Next to the chapel stood the dancing chamber, the scene of song and dance, with minstrelsy and pageantry scarcely surpassed in the royal household itself.

At the southern end of the hall was the kitchen or service block (6), comprising the kitchen itself with its own fireplace and equipped with spits, dressing-tables for preparing meat, and other cooking utensils, together with related domestic offices. The records mention the buttery, with its facilities for receiving and storing wine; the pantry with its bins for storing bread; the bakehouse where the bread was baked; the scullery dealing with the plates, dishes and kitchen utensils; the larder with its storage facilities; the ewery where the ewers, or pitchers used for bringing water for washing the hands, were kept; the saucery, spicery, and chandlery, containing the stocks of condiments, spices and candles respectively required by the establishment. All these were necessary adjuncts of princely living. The finely constructed vault, known as John of Gaunt's cellar (5), which can still be seen, probably formed a storage basement underneath or beyond the kitchen block, and steps from one of its doorways led to the hall. It is doubtful if it ever served as the castle prison or dungeon as was suggested by one of Leicester's early historians.

Another group of buildings had to do with the business side of the establishment. The steward and receiver had separate offices. There was a treasury which acted as a strong-room for money and valuables and as a muniment room for charters, account rolls and other important documents. The castle also had its own prison, quite separate from the town and county gaols, and near by were the gallows which were used for thieves taken on the lord's lands. Incidentally, the borough records include a number of cases of escape and other incidents concerning the prison: in 1305 the prison keeper, when visiting the prison, accidentally tripped against the iron door, fell and broke his neck; in 1309 three men entered the gate of the castle, broke the door of the prison and attacked five brothers imprisoned there, actually killing one of them. Lastly, there were various stables and miscellaneous buildings at the castle, the remaining space within the enclosure being taken up by gardens (16). The castle mill (8) stood on the river just below and the chief forester of Leicester Forest had a house near by.

The household which occupied the castle from time to time was an extremely large and costly organization which was often augmented by varying numbers of guests. Edward I, Edward II and Edward III all stayed at the castle and extant accounts for 1313–14 show that household expenses amounted to nearly £8,000 in that year. That Leicester tradesmen benefited is shown by a list giving details of fish, pigs, meat, hay, sheep and wine purchased for this year. Thomas of Lancaster enjoyed a reputation for princely extravagance and under John of Gaunt the splendour and magnitude of the household vied with that of the king himself. Hunting parties such as that described by the monk Knighton in 1390, when the king and queen and the greatest lords and ladies in the land were at the castle, represented the height of luxury and display.

But the castle represented more than princely extravagance. It served as the administrative centre of the Midland estates of the honor of Leicester, and from Earl Edmund's time it came to be used by the king's justices as a court of assize, a use which has continued right down to the present time. It also symbolized the lord's authority over the borough of Leicester. In recognition of this, it became customary for the mayor, after his election, to go to the castle to swear an oath of allegiance before the lord's steward, an occasion marked by a costly dinner which the mayor provided. A detailed procedure for the ceremony was laid down at the beginning of the seventeenth century, and with the exception of an occasion in 1766 when the mayor refused to acknowledge the superior authority of the Duchy of Lancaster in this way, the ceremony was repeated year by year until the castle passed to the county justices.

With the accession of John of Gaunt's son, Henry IV, the honor and castle of Leicester, as part of the Lancastrian possessions, became an appanage of the Crown and the castle entered upon a period of decline and decay. Even so its former prestige was occasionally revived; Henry IV and Henry V stayed there, the Parliament of Bats in 1426 assembled in the castle hall and Henry VI, Edward IV and Richard III were also visitors.

During the first half of the fifteenth century, hardly a year passed without some appreciable expenditure on its fabric. Between 1417 and 1423, for instance, wall building on a fairly extensive scale was undertaken, and in 1422–3 the southern or Turret Gateway (13) connecting with the enclosure of the Newarke foundation was built. This gateway is now only partially preserved, having been largely destroyed during an election squabble in 1832, but originally it had an arched entrance passage and lodge with a portcullis chamber and other rooms on the upper floor, and small angular turrets flanking the south side. Later, after a fire in 1444, a large new house and other apartments were built at the main entrance to the castle and it is most probable that the present gateway and house standing near to the north door of St Mary's church can be identified with this reconstruction(9). Nevertheless, with the exception of the 'estate office' rooms located there, the castle became increasingly neglected and the last authentic record of its occupation, other than by officials of the honor, is a letter written by Richard III "from my castle of Leicester" on 18 August 1483.

During the sixteenth century royal commissioners surveyed it from time to time, but it seems doubtful whether the repairs they recommended were ever carried out. John Leland for instance, visiting Leicester in 1536, commented that the castle was "a thing of smaul estimation" with "no appearance either of high walls or ditches" and a hundred years later Charles I authorized the sale of certain parts of the buildings which had – according to a survey – become "utterly ruynous, useless & irreparable".

Turning to its later history, during the Civil War Leicester took the side of Parliament against the Crown and in May 1645 was attacked by Charles I and Prince Rupert. The castle, with its defences hastily improvised, was captured and the town itself surrendered and was fined as a punishment. It was recaptured by the Parliamentarians after the battle of Naseby, and the castle and honor were contracted for sale. This was soon nullified, for with the restoration of the monarchy all lands confiscated or sold were returned to their owners. The castle thus became Crown property again and from time to time its buildings (except the hall) were leased to the person holding the office of constable.

From the end of the seventeenth century the castle's history centres chiefly on the hall which "tho' it has been dismantled and made unfit for any warlike matters'' – so wrote a contemporary – ''yet it is of use to the county for the keeping of the assizes twice a year''. During the reign of William and Mary the eastern side of it was taken down and replaced by a brick front, and shortly afterwards the old kitchen was converted into a coach-house. Apart from its use as a court, the hall was occasionally the scene of special functions, such as the ball held there in 1722 or the grand concert in 1774. These were possible because, although fitted up for the holding of courts, the interior of the hall still remained undivided. In fact, as a visitor at that time observed, it was ''so lofty and spacious that at the assizes, the courts are so far distant from one another, as not to disturb each other''. At the beginning of the last century it was divided into two separate courts, a civil and a criminal court, with an entrance lobby between, and a grand jury room above. A barristers' room was built at the end of the hall on the site of the old kitchen block, and about the same time the building now known as the Castle House was added to the old gatehouse (9).

In 1888 the county justices purchased the castle from the Crown, thus terminating its long connection with the Duchy of Lancaster. The hall still remains the central feature and at the present time is used for the Assizes, the Quarter Sessions, the County Court and other judicial functions. The Gate House and Castle House are now private residences, and the area between the castle and the river has been laid out as a public park known as the Castle Gardens. This has not only made possible the preservation of the remains of wall foundations (15) but has also served to draw attention to, and enhance, the historical interest and beauty of the castle site and its remaining buildings.

Suggested reading

G. T. Clark, *Medieval Military Architecture in England*, 1884.

Levi Fox, *The Administration of the Honor of Leicester in the Fourteenth Century*, 1940.

Levi Fox, *Leicester Castle*, 1944.

William Kelly, *Royal Progresses and Visits to Leicester*, 1884.

William Napier Reeve, *Chronicles of the Castle and of the Earls of Leicester*, 1867.

James Thompson, *Account of Leicester Castle*, 1859.

3

Church life in medieval Leicester

The period that we call the Middle Ages lasted a thousand years, from the end of Roman rule in Western Europe to that age of geographical discovery and intellectual uproar that called itself the Renaissance. It was a millennium that made a new society out of the wreckage of the ancient world, subdued the forests and the fens of the North, bred the languages that we use today out of Latin and the ancient Germanic stock, shaped a new civilization in Europe – our own. It was an age of intense activity in countryside and town, and important as the Christian Church was in all that was said and much that was done, a study of ecclesiastical life in medieval Leicester might seem to approach that long period in the city's history in a narrow and restrictive fashion. Medieval Leicester had more than its churches, more than its castle and walls; it had streets, houses, markets, fields, and, above all, people. People may be seen at their best in church, but are they necessarily seen at their most characteristic? Medieval Leicestrians may have gone to church more often than some of their successors do – let us say for the sake of argument that they did – but only a handful of them actually lived there. Shall we not miss a great deal of the city's daily life if we peer at it through a stained-glass window? The answer, oddly, is no, not very much.

In the first place the Church's commanding place in medieval society was very obviously expressed by its buildings. We marvel even today, in an age that has learned to build with steel, at the architectural splendour of the great cathedrals, and in their own time the spires and steeples of medieval churches towered above the other works of man. In such a town as Leicester, a huddle of timber houses and thatched roofs, only the castle stood out for the secular world, and the castle was matched by St Mary's Abbey, and outnumbered by the other churches. The quality and sophistication of its architecture set the Church apart, and so did its furnishings. There were rich churches and poor churches. When Geoffrey le Mason and his friends stole ornaments and vestments from St Leonard's in 1297 they got only a sacrilegious three shillings' worth. Henry VIII, on the other hand, made £1,000 from the lead roofs of St Mary's Abbey alone; but between such extremes as these the churches and their services brought colour and opulence and a show of drama into a world that was, by our comfortable standards, grim and harsh and poor.

The medieval Church's primacy, however, lay in more than its command of wealth and skill, even though it disposed of resources that were proportionately greater, in terms of what society had to offer, than those of the modern State. It both reflected and shaped the institutions of the secular world, sharing talent and experience with the State, instructing and supporting the great lords who patronized it, drawing its own strength from the laity who obeyed it. It offered the spiritual service of prayer and intercession to all, and its temporal skills to those who could afford them. Every word that has come down to us from the Middle Ages was written by the clergy or their pupils: we have no choice but to study medieval society in their terms.

We know nothing precise about the beginnings of Christianity in Leicester, but there were bishops here, ministering to the Middle Anglian tribes, from the middle of the seventh century. It is most unlikely that their cathedral was where St Martin's church stands, although St Martin's has an early dedication and it was the chief parish church of the medieval borough of Leicester (14).* As Leicester never does things by halves, we have two other possible sites for the pre-Conquest cathedral: St Nicholas' (18) and St Mary de Castro (17). On political grounds St Mary's might seem the better candidate; its predecessor was a collegiate church of unknown origins, and its association with the castle suggests a similar association with some pre-Conquest centre of government. St Nicholas', on the other hand, has a strong archaeological claim; its nave is very early work, and its connection with the Jewry Wall shows that it was a church of unusual size and importance raised in the ruins of a Roman city. If it was not built for a bishop, and that was a time when parish churches as we know them did not exist, then there were some interesting goings-on in Mercian Leicester. Mercian, because the bishop's authority, like that of the ephemeral archbishopric of Lichfield, depended upon the power of the Mercian kings. There was a time in the ninth century when the diocese of Leicester stretched as far as Dorchester-on-Thames in Oxfordshire, the heart of the first West Saxon kingdom, but then it vanished, with much else, in the darkness of the Danish invasions.

When the light returns, we find five Danish armies settled in the wreckage of Mercia, where their chief camps, the famous five boroughs of Derby, Leicester, Lincoln, Nottingham, and Stamford, became busy

*The numbers in brackets refer to Map 3, Medieval Leicester (page 30).

centres of trade and administration. Leicester had a dependent shire, but
had lost its diocese, which was absorbed into the huge see of Lincoln.
One consequence of that absorption was that Oxford now lay in the
diocese of Lincoln, and when a university developed there in the twelfth
century it was able to grow without constant interference from its
bishop – an important historical accident. In Leicester the Bishop of
Lincoln was not only closer to hand, he was also a local landowner,
whose estate, later known as the Bishop's Fee, appears in Domesday Book
as a substantial tract of farmland to the east and south of the walled town,
and included a church where St Margaret's now stands (15). The Domesday survey was concerned only with landholders and taxpayers, and its
references to churches are incidental or inferential, but it appears that by
1086, when Domesday Book was compiled, there were six churches in
the walled town, amongst which we can at least number St Mary's,
St Nicholas', and All Saints', All Hallows (11), a dedication which seems
always to indicate a church established before the Conquest.

This is a point at which our interest in the churches is a particularly
useful guide to the history of the town. In 1086 a large part of Leicester –
some 200 of the 300-odd recorded houses – was in the hands of a Norman
lord, Hugh de Grentmesnil. Hugh and his son Ivo were turbulent men and
rebels, and Ivo was constrained to mortgage his estate, When Ivo died on
crusade, his mortgagee Robert de Beaumont succeeded him. By royal
favour and a lucky marriage of his daughter he then secured the lordship
of the whole town, and probably the title of Earl of Leicester which he
passed on to his son. Robert celebrated his rising fortunes in 1107 by
founding a college in the grounds of the castle, in the church we call St
Mary de Castro, and endowing it with, among other property, all the
churches in Leicester.

Now it is certain that the patronage of those churches was not originally
in the hands of a single lord. A cluster of churches in an old town, in a
town like Leicester, Huntingdon, or Cambridge, is a sign that there we
have a mercantile settlement that developed before the twelfth century.
Conversely, an old town that is contained by a single parish – Boston is a
good example – is usually a town which made its money after 1100. In the
Middle Ages successful men liked to found churches – the patronage of a
living showed that a man had substance and a following, as well as pious
instincts – but after 1100 the consolidation of the Church's territorial
rights, into the units that we call parishes, made it difficult even for great
men to upset the existing pattern. Multiple churches, therefore, appeared
only where wealth was spread fairly evenly in the community at an early
date; in the late Anglo-Saxon or early Norman borough, in other words.

That was the condition of Leicester immediately after the Conquest.
The churches duly appear, but so do the Norman governors, and in

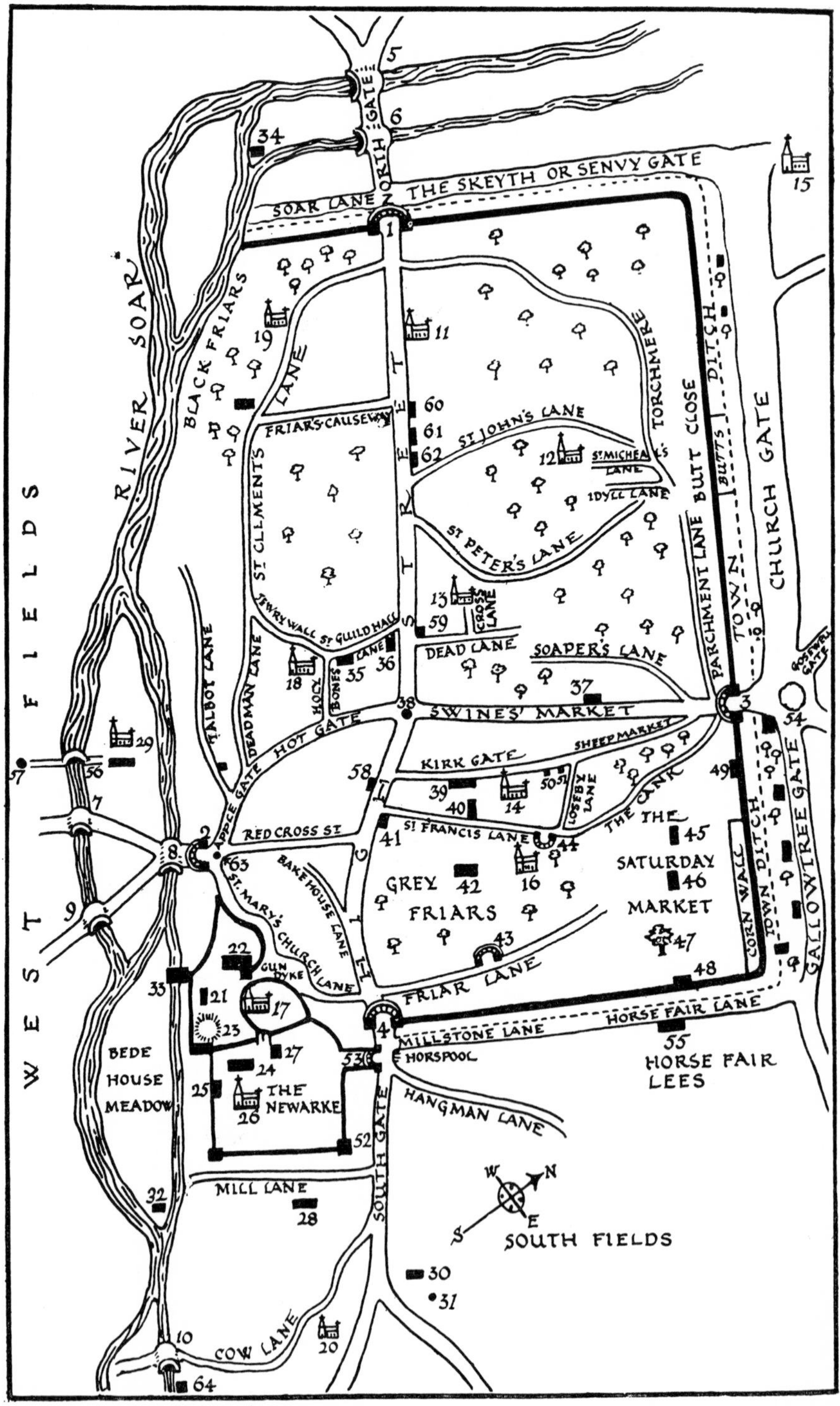

Map 3   Medieval Leicester

Leicester Robert de Beaumont came to exercise an unusual power. The English kings usually kept the lordship of the larger towns in their own hands, but Leicester was handed over to its earls, and came back to the Crown only when the earldom itself returned as an appendage of the Duchy of Lancaster. Robert was an ambitious and vigorous man, and he evidently scooped up the patronage of the city churches with the other property that he accumulated. He then transferred it to his new college of St Mary's, a community appointed to pray for his soul and the souls of his parents and kinsmen, and also to provide clerks, chaplains and counsellors for his household and estates. Some 30 years later, in 1143, Earl Robert the Hunchback improved upon his father's design. He set up a house of Augustinian canons, known as the Abbey of the Assumption of St Mary,

---

Key to Map 3

1	North Gate	33	Castle Mill
2	West Gate	34	North Mill
3	East Gate	35	Old Mayor's Hall
4	South Gate	36	Blue Boar Inn
5	North Bridge	37	Lord's Place
6	Frogmire Bridge	38	High Cross
7	Bow Bridge	39	Guildhall
8	West Bridge	40	Wigston's Hospital
9	Braunston Bridge	41	Henry Costeyn's house
10	Cow Bridge	42	The Grey Friars' priory
11	All Saints' church	43	Grey Friars' Gateway
12	St Michael's church	44	Grey Friars' Gateway
13	St Peter's church	45	Shambles and Drapery
14	St Martin's church	46	The Gainsborough
15	St Margaret's church	47	Elm tree
16	Grey Friars' church	48	Green Dragon Inn
17	St Mary's church	49	Angel Inn
18	St Nicholas' church	50	Maiden Head Inn
19	St Clement's church	51	St George's gildhall
20	St Sepulchre's church	52	Rupert's Tower
21	Castle Hall	53	Magazine Gateway
22	Castle House	54	Bere Hill
23	Castle Mound	55	Old Barn
24	Newarke Hospital	56	Little Bow Bridge
25	Dean of Newarke's house	57	St Austin's Well
26	Newarke College church	58	Roger Wigston's (?) house
27	Wigston's chantry house	59	Free Grammar School
28	Newarke Grange	60	Shirehall
29	The Austin Friars	61	Prisona Regis
30	Hermitage	62	St John's Hospital
31	St Sepulchre's Well	63	Red Cross
32	Newarke Mill	64	Mary Mill

in the meadows north of the town, endowed it with the college's lands, and delivered the government of the college to it as well (Map 4: see left-hand edge). What the priests of the college thought of the arrangement is not recorded, but we can guess. They were the victims of a significant change in ecclesiastical fashion and the patterns of lay patronage – one of several, as we shall see, in the Middle Ages.

The twelfth century saw the dazzling success of the Cistercian Order, a movement for the reform and strict observance of the monastic life that was begun by a handful of Burgundian monks at Cîteaux. The Cistercians tried to escape from the snares of lay society, but they were remorselessly pursued by their would-be benefactors, so that their houses grew richer and richer until they were caught in the very bonds of proprietorial authority that the reformers had tried to avoid. The rest of the Church watched the process with mixed feelings, but it was clear that monastic rules were at a premium, and the Augustinian order was an attractive compromise. The Augustinians were priests who were bound by monastic vows, but who were not thereby prevented, as the monks were, from engaging in pastoral work outside their abbeys and priories. Earl Robert II founded a Cistercian abbey at Garendon, but he evidently thought that his father's plans would be better realized by a new establishment in Leicester, richer and more ambitiously housed than the college in the castle, but also more strictly governed. St Mary's-in-the-Meadows was the consequence.

Robert's friends and dependents joined him in endowing the house, and it became one of the richest in its order. The abbey is familiar to many students of history who have no particular knowledge of Leicester, because in the fourteenth century it produced a famous chronicler, Henry of Knighton, and because the catalogue of its well-stocked library has survived, although we now have only a dozen of its thousand manuscript books. Yet we know comparatively little of the ordinary life of the abbey. What we do know suggests that it did not develop quite as Earl Robert had hoped, and that in a sense his larger schemes were out of date before they were realized. The canons were given too many churches for them to man by themselves, and if they were constrained to appoint other clergy to them, as they were, their own potentialities were wasted. They evidently concentrated upon conventual affairs, administered their estates, built up their library, and celebrated divine office, as all religious houses did, night and day, year upon year, century upon century. But the future of the Church as a social force did not lie with the enclosed orders. By the thirteenth century it lay rather with the friars, who worked among the growing populations of the towns, and with the universities, who were already training a new kind of clerical administrator, skilled in dialectic and the right use of written memoranda. And there was also to be a larger place for the parochial clergy themselves, aided in their pastoral work and personally enriched (the fortunate ones) by the laity's growing taste for social gilds, which needed chaplains, and for chantries, private foundations for the continual celebration of masses and commemorative services.

We should expect these changes to be reflected in Leicester, and we find them here with those differences which make local history worth studying. The town suffered a good deal between the late eleventh and the early fourteenth century from the turbulence of its lords: every man, as Lady Bracknell said, should have a hobby, and the earls of Leicester's was rebellion. The most celebrated of them, Simon de Montfort, had little to do with the town and caused it no particular harm when he was killed at Evesham, but on several other occasions, in 1173 and 1329 especially, Leicester was ravaged by royal forces and its lord's private enemies. Two parishes, in the north-eastern and north-western corners of the walled town, St Michael's and St Clement's (12 and 19), never seem to have recovered from the sack of 1173; they certainly contained much open ground in later centuries, and their churches decayed and vanished. So did St Peter's, by Freeschool Lane, perhaps for the same reason (13). The other parish churches, however, gradually grew in size and elaboration, led by St Martin's and St Margaret's. St Martin's was a large church, even before its Victorian restoration, and its chapels accommodated two important town gilds, St George's and the gild of Corpus Christi, founded in 1343. These were social and religious clubs, but the gild of Corpus Christi was closely associated with the governing body of the town, and its gildhall therefore survived the Reformation to serve in later centuries as a town hall. It is still in use today, as a museum, library, and occasional theatre; functions that are not far removed in social terms from its original purposes. These foundations, and those in the other churches, like the gild of St Margaret and St Katherine in St Margaret's, are signs of the increasing sophistication and, in absolute terms, the prosperity of the burghal community. For various reasons, its political history among them, Leicester was a place of less consequence by the fifteenth century than it had been in the eleventh and twelfth, but it was still able to rebuild and enrich its churches. In them, new aisles and chapels provided a setting for increasingly elaborate services, whilst the laity used them for every kind of social and public meeting. Parishioners would meet in church not only to attend services, but to pay debts, strike bargains, and hold gilds. They furnished them as they might furnish their own prized properties, and they equipped them with chantries to secure their welfare beyond the grave. The gilds and the chantries, for privately- or corporately-endowed masses, were the burgesses' versions of the religious houses that the nobility had founded in the twelfth century. Its earls gave Leicester a college of priests and an abbey, and two small hospitals for lepers and

other chronic invalids, St Leonard's outside the North Gate, and St John
the Baptist in Belgrave Gate. During the thirteenth century Simon de
Montfort and other benefactors had set up three houses of friars, the
Dominicans, or Black Friars, the Augustinians (29), and the Franciscans,
or Grey Friars (42), who specialized in missionary work in the towns.
Now in the fourteenth century a new period of aristocratic patronage
began which in turn, as we shall see, stimulated a response from the
townsmen. In 1331, Earl Henry of Lancaster, second son of the prince to
whom Leicester had passed after de Montfort's fall, founded a chapel,
clergyhouse, infirmary, and almshouse in a fortified enclosure to the
south-east of the castle. The whole was dedicated to the honour of God
and the Virgin Mary, and it was known formally as the Hospital of the
Annunciation of St Mary in the Newarke (24). Earl Henry was ageing and
blind, and he had had an adventurous and over-exciting political career
that was not of his own choosing; he wished to use his means for the
salvation of his soul and the common good, and to provide a decent, that is
to say a suitably imposing, burial place for himself and his heirs. He lived,
probably to his own surprise, until 1345. When he died his son, Henry of
Derby, was already fighting in France as a trusted captain of Edward III,
and within a few years Derby had deservedly risen so high in the king's
favour as a military commander and a counsellor that he was made first
duke of Lancaster. In 1355 he re-established his father's hospital on a
princely scale, with a new collegiate church (26) to enshrine the reli-
quary of a thorn from Christ's crown of thorns, a treasure bestowed upon
him in admiration by the king of France himself. All that remains of that
complex of buildings today is the so-called Magazine Gateway in the
Newarke (53) and part of the Trinity Hospital, but for almost 200 years it
was a brilliant centre of religious and social life, a place of pilgrimage for
the devout, and a constant and flourishing reminder of the favour in which
the house of Lancaster – after Duke Henry, his son-in-law, John of Gaunt,
and after Duke John, his son King Henry IV, and his successors – held the
town.

It would be unrealistic to suppose that all these blessings were unani-
mously welcomed by the townsmen. Leicester's history as a centre of
nonconformity began long before the birth of its great dissenting congre-
gations, and in the late fourteenth century we find some of the burgesses,
and at one point the Corporation itself, in the heady and dangerous
company of heretics, those who challenged the teaching and judgment of
the Church. We know a good deal about the episode, partly because it
occurred while Knighton was writing his chronicle at St Mary's, but also
because it became part of a movement that threatened the whole structure
of the Church more than a century before the Protestant Reformation.

The extraneous influence came from Oxford, where in the late 1370s a canon of St Mary's, Philip Repton or Repyngdon, was studying divinity and lecturing, and where John Wycliffe, the most celebrated teacher of his day, was drifting away from orthodoxy, and threatening to carry his pupils with him, Repton among them. It seems likely that Repton, who preached Wycliffe's new philosophical teachings widely, brought them back to Leicester, and it is certain that they were sympathetically received, whether or not they were wholly understood, by two influential preachers in the town. One was a layman, an eccentrically devout man called William Smith, who unfriendly gossip said had been driven into celibacy, piety, and ultimately literacy, by his failure to persuade a girl to marry him. Smith established himself in a disused chapel at the hospital in Belgrave Gate to preach and instruct, and there he was joined by a chaplain and sometime-hermit called William Swynderby. Their preaching apparently concentrated upon the shortcomings of the clergy and the abuses and corruption of lay and clerical society, and they gathered a substantial following amongst the townsmen. By 1382 their success provoked the Bishop of Lincoln to move against them, but there is no doubt that the ecclesiastical authorities were chiefly perturbed by the academic movement that had encouraged them, through Repton's agency. If the graduate clergy were once convinced by Wycliffe's arguments against transubstantiation, and so against the peculiar powers and privileges of the priesthood, the whole status of the Church would be imperilled, and the disaffection of the laity would follow as a matter of course. In the end, energetic action by the Archbishop of Canterbury suppressed Wycliffe's teaching and Lollardy, as the new movement was called, in the universities, and the other Lollards could then be left to intermittent but increasingly severe persecution by their bishops.

Most of the academics recanted their opinions, and Repton himself came back to Leicester to be Abbot of St Mary's before he was elevated to the bishopric of Lincoln in 1404. His presence in the abbey no doubt spoiled Knighton's treatment of the events in Belgrave Gate, but as diocesan he certainly obstructed the authorities' later efforts to have Wycliffe's bones exhumed at Lutterworth, where he had died as rector in 1384. We know nothing more about William Smith, but Swynderby had an active and highly dangerous career as a Lollard missionary. At the first of the two ecclesiastical trials which he survived, he was able to produce a testimonial from Leicester, under the common seal of the borough. It was not the best of defences against doctrinal accusations, but it was something.

Smith and Swynderby are worth pondering for several reasons. They stand out as individuals in an age in which much of our knowledge is general and formal. They speak of traditional and enduring grievances, of a kind that are often and naturally muted or misrepresented in official records. Their eccentricities, clament denunciations, and dream of a communal life might remind us of critics of our own society. They save us, in any case, from the assumption that life in the past was less flawed or complicated than our own contrivances. The institutions that they denounced, however, endured some time longer, and we cannot say with confidence that Smith and Swynderby would be better pleased with what they found if they returned to us now. There were, however, some other and different signs of social concern in late medieval Leicester, and they recall us to the theme of patronage and charitable endowment.

Between 1521 and 1526 William Wigston, a rich wool merchant of an influential Leicester family, who had already established a private chantry in the Newarke college, founded a chapel and almshouse on a site by St Martin's churchyard (40). Its charitable purposes allowed the hospital to survive the religious changes of Henry VIII's and Edward VI's reigns, and in the middle of the century it absorbed another endowment, for the maintenance of a grammar school. The city still benefits by Wigston's gifts, but his hospital is also worth attention as an object lesson from his time. It was undoubtedly inspired by the aristocratic examples of the Newarke: Wigston had no sons, but he had a coat-of-arms, and a strong family pride. We know something of his background from the panels of stained-glass rescued in the last century from that deeply interesting house of his brother's, 18 High Cross Street, and preserved today by our excellent city museum. In the representations of the corporal acts of mercy we can see the Wigstons and their fellow-burgesses as they saw themselves – prosperous but compassionate men, second to none in the comfortable appointment of their daily lives, but also alive to their social, or their religious, responsibilities – they would not have recognized the distinction. It may be an idealized portrait, but it was not an ignoble ideal, and although its buildings were wantonly destroyed in the late nineteenth century, Wigston's foundation has lasted longer than either St Mary's Abbey or the great Lancastrian college in the Newarke. That is only one test of an institution's quality, but an institution that is not adaptable is apt to waste its other excellence.

It is common knowledge in Leicester that a few years after the hospital's endowment Thomas Wolsey, cardinal, papal legate, and Archbishop of York, came to Leicester Abbey to rest and to die. The cardinal lies somewhere under the Abbey Park, though not necessarily where the ornate marker now stands amid the imaginative reconstruction of the abbey ruins. In his death, disgraced and helpless, he was a symbol not only of the hollowness of his own ambitions, but of the coming convulsion of his Church. For almost a thousand years the Church had been the mainstay of the State in England, and if it had not been the stronger, it had certainly been the more sophisticated, the better-found, of the partners. Now it was caught in the toils of its own success, and it had a heavy price to pay, at least in wordly terms, to ensure its future. In less than 20 years the monasteries were dissolved, the gilds and chantries suppressed, and all churches, large and small, stripped of their treasures. The reaction of Mary's reign brought bitter strife, and confirmed the country in Protestantism and a powerful national pride. Yet the old forms could not be swept entirely away; not only did the Church of England consciously maintain the administrative and pastoral tradition of its medieval original, but it continually enriched lay society with its old inheritance. It is this particularly that lends point and interest to our study of the Middle Ages, when so many of our institutions struggled to life. The Renaissance was an enlargement of, not a reaction against, medieval experience, just as the astonishing achievements of our industrial society owe their patterns to all that went before. The Middle Ages are with us still: we can contemplate them patronizingly or sympathetically or respectfully, but if we wish to understand medieval man, medieval Leicester, or medieval England, we must go first to church and consider them there.

Suggested reading

Mary Bateson, ed., *Records of the Borough of Leicester*, vols 1 and 2, *1103–1509*, 1899, 1901.

C. J. Billson, *Medieval Leicester*, 1920.

James Crompton, 'Leicester Lollards', *Transactions of the Leicestershire Archaeological and Historical Society*, XLIV, 1968–9, 11–44.

M. D. Knowles, *The Religious Orders in England*, 1948.

W. A. Pantin, *The English Church in the Fourteenth Century*, 1955.

A. Hamilton Thompson, *The Abbey of St Mary of the Meadows, Leicester*, 1949.

A. Hamilton Thompson, *The English Clergy in the later Middle Ages*, 1947.

Victoria History of the County of Leicester, vol. 4, 1958.

4

Leicester and its markets: the seventeenth century

Everyone in Leicester should be interested in its history as a market-town. For many centuries the markets of Leicester were the principal function of its existence, and they are still very important. Today it is said to have the largest retail market in Britain, with more than 400 stalls, three days a week, every week of the year. To visitors from other parts of the country, and indeed from abroad, this is the one thing that always strikes them about our city. I have known Americans and Italians who have come to Leicester specially to spend a day in the market, and take presents and bargains back with them to their friends at home.

Leicester of course is only one of a number of market-towns that existed in our county in the seventeenth century. Altogether there were about 760 markets in England as a whole at that time, and 17 or 18 in Leicestershire itself. Several of these Leicestershire places are still familiar to us as towns today – places like Melton Mowbray, Ashby-de-la-Zouch, and Market Harborough, for instance. Others, like Hallaton and Billesdon, are now no more than villages; they are among the many lost market-towns of England. But Leicester was always by far the most important town in the shire, of course. Though it probably numbered no more than about 4,000 people in 1600, and less than 7,000 in 1700, it was several times as large as any other town in Leicestershire. What is more, during the seventeenth and eighteenth centuries, its importance as a market was undoubtedly increasing. Stage by stage it was attracting a lot of trade away from the smaller towns like Hallaton and Billesdon, until eventually these places died out completely as centres of commerce, whilst Leicester continually expanded.

Nowadays, for most of us, the market in Leicester no doubt means the market-place in front of the old Corn Exchange; or else, for farmers and stock-dealers, the livestock market on the Welford Road. The Welford Road market in fact dates only from 1872, until when all the buying and selling of sheep, cattle, and horses, as well as retail goods, was done in the old town centre. The retail market that we still know today is far more ancient than that in the Welford Road. Nobody quite knows exactly when it originated; but it certainly goes back to the early thirteenth century, when probably it was founded by one of the earls of Leicester (it was often called the Earl's Market), who were influential figures in the trading development of the town as well as in its politics. Leicester's present market, then, has been held every week, on the same site, and the same day – Saturday – for more than 700 years.

Strange though it may seem, however, Leicester's market-place today is not the original one in the town. From the thirteenth century until well into the nineteenth, the name of the present market was the Saturday Market (Map 3). In other words, only the market that was held on Saturday itself was originally held on this site. It was not until Queen Victoria's reign that the other markets, those held on Wednesday and Friday, were transferred to the spot that we know as the Market Place.

The story of Leicester's other markets is a complicated one, but it is most interesting to unravel. Quite a number of towns in England have, like Leicester, more than one medieval market-place. King's Lynn in Norfolk, for example, and Malmesbury and Devizes in Wiltshire each have two. Northampton has had as many as three distinct market-places during its long history, two at least before the present one; and Canterbury has had four or five. But no English town that I know of has had more than Leicester, and I suspect very few people in Leicester realize this fact either. We have certainly the traces, in Leicester, of at least six market-places embedded in our present-day street plan, all originating at different dates and for different reasons.

Let us look for a moment at Maps 3 and 4. We can disentangle quite a lot from some of the street-names of the town, both past and present. Many of the most interesting street names in central Leicester have vanished, or have been altered, it is true. We no longer have (as we used to) an Ironmongers' Row, a Glovers' Row, a Shoemakers' Row, a Swinesmarket, a Parchment Lane, or a Drapery. But still a good number survive, and amongst the most interesting ones, I want to single out five: Red Cross Street, High Cross Street, Woodgate, East Gates and the

Map 4   Map of Leicester dated 1741

Haymarket, and Horsefair Street. Each of these names points us to a former market-place and has its own peculiar history.

Most of us probably think of the space round the Clock Tower as the centre of Leicester today. But it has not always been so. In fact it lies outside the walls of the old borough, as they existed from Roman times down to the eighteenth century. One of the interesting themes in the topographical history of Leicester is that its commercial life has continually tended, over the last 1,800 years, to move further and further east.

Where then was the original centre? The oldest market-place in Leicester that we know of is probably the Roman forum, near St Nicholas' church (Map 1). How long after the Roman occupation the forum remained in use, no one can say. But it is an interesting fact that until the late seventeenth century, the principal meat-market of Leicester was still being held very close to this ancient site, along the former Applegate Street and St Nicholas Street. When and how this meat-market originated we cannot be sure, but it was certainly very ancient, and was possibly the original pre-Conquest market-place of Leicester. In all probability the piles of bones which gave their name to the street so strangely called "Holy Bones" were simply the refuse, over many centuries, from the butchers' shambles near by. Further down Applegate Street, at its junction with Red Cross Street, once stood the old cross which marked the centre of this ancient market, and which gave its name to Red Cross Street (Map 3, 63).

The name of High Cross Street, like Red Cross Street, is also an indication of a former market, and indeed it may well be older in origin than that at the Red Cross. Throughout the medieval period, the commercial heart of Leicester was at the High Cross, which stood until 1773 at the junction of High Cross Street and High Street (Map 3, 38). One last relic of this historic High Cross, a single pillar of it as it was rebuilt in Queen Elizabeth's reign, still survives, and is now standing in the garden of the Newarke Houses Museum. This market at the High Cross is the origin of both the Wednesday and Friday markets, though Wednesday was the original day and Friday was probably not added till the fourteenth or fifteenth century.

This High Cross of Leicester was at the natural route-centre of the old walled town. High Cross Street and Southgate Street formed the original London road through Leicester to the North, until the modern London road took its place in the seventeenth century. In all probability, therefore, the market at the High Cross arose spontaneously and naturally at this point, simply because country people were meeting there to exchange their goods. There was no specific royal grant for it, as there had to be for the markets of most other towns. In technical language it was a 'prescriptive market': that is, the legal right of the townsmen to hold a market at the High Cross lay in the simple fact of its antiquity – in the fact that it had been held there ever "since the memory of man ran not to the contrary", to use the lawyer's phrase.

How far back does this mean the High Cross market existed? We can trace it in documents certainly back to the twelfth century, and probably to a reference in Domesday Book in 1086; but in my view it had most likely existed for a very long time before that date. Its antiquity is confirmed by the fact that it was always, in later centuries, regarded as the traditional meeting-place of the community. The mart itself was spoken of as 'the townsmen's market' or 'the market of the community'. These are significant phrases. Even as late as the eighteenth or nineteenth century, moreover, all public proclamations in Leicester had to be read at the High Cross, and the great fairs of the borough could not begin until they had been formally proclaimed there by the mayor and Corporation, at the end of a long procession round the town, robed in their official scarlet gowns.

All these three ancient markets of Leicester that I have mentioned so far – the High Cross, the Red Cross, and the Saturday Market – lay within the old walled area of the city. The interesting thing about the three other markets is that they all lay just outside the old walled town. It is not difficult to pick out the limits of this walled area on the maps. It is marked by the straight lines of Sanvey Gate and Soar Lane to the north, Churchgate and Gallowtree Gate to the east, and Horsefair Street and Millstone Lane to the south, all of which followed the town ditch outside the Romano-Medieval walls. The direct line of these streets is the more striking because of the confused maze of lanes in the rest of central Leicester.

If Leicester already had three medieval market-places, we may ask, why was it found necessary to develop several new ones as well, outside this walled area? The underlying economic reason was the expansion of trade within the constricted urban area inside the walls, which amounted to no more than 160 acres. In the origins of each new market, however, a variety of other causes was also at work. To the north of the town, outside the North Gate, the wood-market developed because this was the route into the town from Leicester Forest, in which the townsmen had certain fuel-rights. This is the reason for the name Woodgate today, the street leading from the forest to the wood-market of the townsmen.

To the south of the town, just outside the wall again, a patch of land belonging to the Corporation, near the present town hall, came to form a convenient site for the expanding horse-fairs and horse-markets of the borough. In the seventeenth century Leicester was famous for its horse-fairs, especially for the great shire-horses bred in the county, reputedly the most powerful draught-animals in England. For a horse-fair, however, a good deal of space is needed; horses cannot be confined in narrow pens like sheep, and buyers and sellers must have room to see them exercised. This was the reason why in the sixteenth century the horse-fairs came to be held outside the walls. Later, in the eighteenth century, the sheep-market too was transferred to the Horse Fair site. Finally, when both horse- and sheep-markets had been moved further out of the town, the area was turned into a garden, the new town hall was built along one side of it, and it was renamed Town Hall Square. But the name of Horsefair Street still reminds us of one of Leicester's most noted features in the seventeenth and eighteenth centuries, the great age of horse-traffic in England.

The last market, that held outside the East Gates, and still commemorated in the street called the Haymarket (Map 5), is in some ways the most interesting of all. The name Haymarket itself dates only from the eighteenth century, when, with the great increase in Leicester's horse-trade, it was found necessary to move the old haymarket to a more spacious site. As an extra-mural market-place, however, the area round the Clock Tower, in Humberstone Gate, Gallowtree Gate, and the Haymarket, certainly goes back far beyond this time, at least to the mid-thirteenth century. Where the Clock Tower itself now stands, there stood for centuries the old cross of this extra-mural market. It was called the Barrell Cross, which was a corruption of Bere Hill Cross (Map 3, 54). This word 'bere' was another word for barley, and this space was in origin Leicester's barley market. The sacks of grain were placed, week by week, by the country farmers on the hillock around the cross, in order to keep them out of the mire of the unpaved streets of the town.

Nor was this all. Twice a year, for more than a week, every May and October, the great medieval fairs of Leicester had been held in this same area, probably since the fourteenth century. In the sixteenth century two new fairs were started, moreover; in the seventeenth century, at least one and perhaps two further fairs; and in the eighteenth century as many as four new ones. By 1800, then, there were at least nine or ten fairs held every year in Leicester, chiefly for livestock, but also for all sorts of merchandise, and of course for amusements too. The growth in the number of these fairs and the business transacted in them was one of the most important reasons why this area, round the present Clock Tower, tended to become, more and more, the commercial heart of the city. And since fairs at this time often drew buyers and sellers from distant parts of the country, their rapid growth in Leicester is also a striking indication of the town's booming economy as a great market – a market, by the seventeenth century, of much more than local importance.

Why was it that this area round the Clock Tower had become, certainly by the seventeenth century, the principal fair-ground of Leicester? The reasons are of great interest. In the nineteenth century we find that the ground on which many of the stalls of the fair were set up bore the curious name of No Man's Land. Where this name occurs, it is usually an indication of disputed ownership; and in this case it is no doubt a survival from the time when the ownership of much of this area of Leicester's extra-mural suburbs (as they then were) was fiercely contested between the Corporation and the Bishop of Lincoln. It was in St Margaret's parish, and this parish was for long in the hands of the bishops of Lincoln, though the actual jurisdiction over much of it was claimed, with varying success, by the Corporation.

Conditions of this kind on the edge of a town almost always produced a rather lawless kind of community, and they often fostered much greater freedom of trade. This seems to be just what happened at Leicester. In the sixteenth and seventeenth centuries, the Corporation was continually worried by the growth of illicit trading in this area; by the many un-licensed inns springing up in it, where also trade was often carried on; and – worst of all – by the growth of non-conformity in this district. But however annoyed the Corporation might be, it could do very little about it, because the traders and innkeepers themselves claimed to be outside both the Corporation's jurisdiction and that of the county justices – in short in *No Man's Land*.

This was one of the chief local reasons, there can be little doubt, for the growth of fairs and markets along Humberstone Gate and the Hay-market. But there was also another reason: and this was the fact that, during the late sixteenth and seventeenth centuries, the present London road to Leicester, from Market Harborough and along Gallowtree Gate and Belgrave Gate, gradually came to supersede the old London route, from Welford, along Southgate Street and High Cross Street. All over England, the seventeenth century witnessed a dramatic increase in inland traffic of all kinds, especially by waggon and by coach: in Leicester this kind of traffic found great difficulty in negotiating the old gateways and narrow streets of the walled borough. By coming through Harborough and down Gallowtree Gate instead, however, one avoided all such difficulties, and arrived direct at the fair-ground outside the East Gates. It was not until 1774 that the four medieval gates of the town were taken down.

Despite all the changes in Leicester's markets over the centuries, the Market Place that we know has, since the seventeenth century, always held a pre-eminent position as the centre of retail trade in the town, as distinct from trade in corn and livestock. With the diversion of the route from London down Gallowtree Gate, it rapidly expanded at the expense of the older retail market at the High Cross, which thereafter gradually declined in importance. As the walls of the town fell out of use in the seventeenth century, moreover, passageways were cut through them at various points to ease the way into Gallowtree Gate, and the trade of the old Saturday Market flourished as never before. (This is the origin of the alley by Messrs Simpkin and James's shop, and of other alleyways between the Market Place and Gallowtree Gate.)

Most of the travellers of the time who visited Leicester, it is true, were not very impressed by it. One of them, Thomas Baskerville, was even so rude as to call it "an old and stinking city, situated upon a dull river". But although Stuart Leicester had its acute economic problems, the opinions of travellers like Baskerville were usually rather superficial. If they had lived in Leicester for any length of time they would have discovered that its richest townsmen were among the wealthiest of any inland town in England. Some of the probate inventories these men left behind them at their death – the lists of their domestic goods, stock and shopwares – record property worth nearly £2,000, or about £80,000 in modern terms. Quite clearly Stuart Leicester was a town of substantial wealth, and the basis of much of this wealth was its trade as one of the great market centres of the Midlands.

Suggested reading

C. J. Billson, *Medieval Leicester*, 1920.

Victoria History of the County of Leicester, vol. 3, 1955. Sections on 'Industries' and 'Roads'.

Victoria History of the County of Leicester, vol. 4, 1958. Sections on 'Social and Economic History, 1509–1600' by E. J. W. Kerridge; 'Social and Administrative History, 1660–1735' by W. A. Jenkins and C. T. Smith; 'Topography' by R. A. McKinley and Janet Martin (especially section on St Martin's parish).

5

Eighteenth-century Leicester

Edward Bracebridge and Thomas Ludlam were the Chamberlains of Leicester in 1712 – roughly their position was equivalent to the present City Treasurer. When they came to make up their accounts that year they recorded one payment of particular interest: "£12 to Mr Thomas Roberts for his paines in making a survey of the Corporation". It is these "paines" which have given us the first really useful map of the town, though it does not seem to have seen the light of day until 1741 (Map 4). It may well have been in official use for a generation earlier. The first thing which stands out is the small size of the town compared with its present extent. St Margaret's church is in the fields outside the town; the place where the Clock Tower will stand in 150 years' time is on the eastern border of the town; the location of the present town hall is outside too. Incidentally, the map preserves the much earlier medieval tradition of putting the east and not the north at the top so that it is easier to use if turned through 90° clockwise.

Apart from the churches and a sparse handful of buildings, the only thing surviving in Leicester now from the time of the map is the pattern of the streets. This reaches gropingly back towards the possible Roman layout of the town. In 1700 the town was on the brink of growth and some renewal, and it is perhaps helpful here to look at some figures and what they imply.

We have no accurate figure for the population in 1700 (accurate figures are a modern development) but it was probably about 6,000, a bit smaller than Ashby-de-la-Zouch is now and only half the size of Market Harborough. For the first 20 years of the century the numbers rose, then came a plateau which lasted far longer, for 40 years, until, about 1760, they started to rise again. The first census in 1801 gives us the first really accurate figure, and it shows the population as just under 17,000, a little bigger than Melton Mowbray today. This growth to nearly three times its size of a century before caused many changes in the town and advanced

in step with many others. Even so it was nothing like the growth of the
nineteenth century. The town moved then from its 17,000 population to
a total of 210,000 by 1901, multiplying its size not by nearly three but by
nearly 13. Even so the eighteenth century saw not only a considerable
urban renewal but also changes in the outlook and occupation of the
townspeople which laid the basis for the later astronomical growth.

Our main impressions of the streets of the town all through the century
would probably have been smell and dirt, but behind the streets and houses
in many parts the map shows that there were ample and spacious gardens
throughout the town, and it was not until towards the end of the century
that some parts of the old town were being built up by infilling. For
instance, the area now cut through by the Ring Road from the Gyratory
System to St Margaret's was clear then, an area of open gardens traversed
by small lanes curling between High Cross Street, still known and marked
on the map as High Street, and Churchgate. This remained clear of
housing until into the nineteenth century. What largely happened to
absorb the increase in population was a process we are only too familiar
with today. At the end of the seventeenth century roughly one family in
32 had to share a house. By 1801 one family in eight were sharing.
Multiple occupancy was four times as common. However, in the better
parts of the town, round St Martin's and Friar Lane, and with the laying
out of New Street through the land of the old Grey Friary, eliminating the
reputed burial place of Richard III, much rebuilding had taken place, and
some of the houses are still there to show the comfort prosperous
eighteenth-century Leicester families could afford. No. 17 Friar Lane
was probably built about 1750 and, with the pediment over the door, the
flanking pilasters, and round-headed windows, it gives a good idea of mid-
century taste: prosperous and a little heavy. No. 18 High Cross Street
shows a solution to the problem of new building tried towards the end of
the century, where a 'new' eighteenth-century house facing directly on to
the street has been grafted on to the old fifteenth-century house of Roger
Wigston which had stood, in the fashion of medieval houses, end on to the
street. Until recently there was a smaller example of this technique in
Southgate Street where a fifteenth-century house had a new front built on
to its street end, the great oak beams of the old house being lodged
directly into the new eighteenth-century brickwork. This house was
demolished during the clearance for the underpass and was more renowned
as a specialist bootmakers than for its unsuspected architectural interest.
Fortunately the City Council has determined to preserve Roger Wigston's
house, the home of the finest secular stained glass of its period, un-
paralleled in the country, for only one other example of such fifteenth-
century building survives, much disguised, in the centre of the town.

The town must have shown many such buildings, dating from the

Middle Ages, in the eighteenth century and some of them lingered on to give the street scenes which John Flower preserved in his book of *Views of Ancient Buildings in the Town and County of Leicester* published in 1826.

While only a few of the buildings of eighteenth-century Leicester now remain, the question of what Leicester people did for a living can be considered from other sources. Two problems spring to mind at once if we are considering a town's life and growth: first, where did they get their water from; and second, what did they do with their sewage. Failure to deal with either of these matters leaves any community wide open to cholera and typhoid. In Leicester most of the water was obtained from wells scattered throughout the town and there are signs that towards the end of the century the difficulties of drawing water were eased by putting pumps in some of these wells. There was also a civic supply of water. Streams tapped outside the town in the Conduit Street area were brought in pipes to discharge in a building called the Conduit (the little dome-shaped building in the north corner of the Market on Map 4). There was a great civic fuss about this supply at the end of the seventeenth century, and in 1695, after Alderman John Wilkins' bill for the job was disputed, the pipes were broken by saboteurs, and Wilkins and his supporters were thrown off the Corporation. The mechanism both for throwing them off and reinstating them on the Corporation was lengthy and complicated. Much of the water must have run to waste so in 1771 permission was given for a cistern to be let into the ground by the outlet of the Conduit to act as a reservoir and a pump was put with it. Other pumps were at the Gainsborough, roughly in the position the Corn Exchange now occupies, in the Horsefair, at the town gaol, and at the Free Grammar School (now carefully restored as a headquarters by Bartons Transport). The town also took power in 1759 to levy a special rate for putting pumps down at other wells then in existence; and there may be some connection with this sealing of the water supply from some contamination by rubbish with the falling of the death rate which takes place after 1760. There is some evidence that the water table of the town, the level at which water occurs, has fallen since that period, so the possibilities for working wells and pumps are not easily ascertainable from modern conditions.

Scavenging seems to have been done sometimes on contract and sometimes by a Corporation official, but it was usually haphazard. In 1729 the Corporation bought a new cart for the scavenger, though whether he was an official or was merely provided with the cart is not clear. At least there are no payments for his salary, and so he probably made his living by selling what he collected for manure. Again the town had to wait until the public health problems of the vast nineteenth-century population caused widespread epidemic diseases before the problem of sewage disposal was tackled properly.

Improvements in housing and water supply were, however, only one side of things. Transport too was changing as the whole tempo of life all over the country quickened. As far back as 1466 the town had had bye-laws for all householders to be responsible for the upkeep of the streets in front of their own houses. This produced a town neither much better nor much worse than others for getting about in. There were also the seemingly modern problems of obstruction and parking, and on occasions these led to prosecution. In January 1764, for instance, John Clarke was presented at Quarter Sessions for "letting his Waggon stand in the open street called the Gallow tree Gate loaded with Branches of trees, which stood loaded there five days and nights which was a publick Nusance to the Inhabitants of the said Street, was greatly Complained of, and was an Obstruction to the passing and Repassing of the said Street. Several persons attending then and there with a Corpse that was going to be Interred could not pass without great difficulty and danger." Earlier in the century the difficulty and danger could be even greater for at one time the Grand Jury reported "Thomas Toopots and Thomas Hastwell Senior for diging a gravill pit soe big that horse and man may bee spoyled at it and allowing it to lie open it being in the free school laine at the side of my Lords place yard", which fixes the position as just about the corner of Union Street and Freeschool Lane now.

The Corporation tried to improve the state of the roads and on a number of occasions carried out road repair and widening within the town, but the approaches remained very bad until the Turnpike Trusts took over these main roads leading to Leicester. Then there was substantial improvement. The present A6 from Market Harborough to Leicester and Loughborough was improved by turnpiking from 1726, the A50 to Ashby in 1753, the A47 to Hinckley in 1754, the Melton and the Lutterworth Roads in 1764, and the Welford Road last of all in 1765. The Harborough Road was the most crucial as it commanded the way to London. Up to that time the main London road had been via Welford, but as that was not improved until 40 years after the Harborough Road, the traffic was drained across to the Harborough route and the old centre of the town at High Cross was pulled across towards the East Gates, where the present Clock Tower is. There was another factor working to shift the town's centre of gravity: the old town gates themselves. These seriously restricted access to the town as they were very narrow, but the new Harborough Turnpike allowed coaches to pull up at the town without having to squeeze through the gates and the narrow streets within the built-up area. A series of coaching inns developed along Gallowtree Gate and Granby Street to meet the needs of the coaches, and they flourished until the coming of the railways. In 1773–4 the gates at last came down (the Corporation sold them only on the condition that the purchasers demolished them). Conveyance to the town of bulk cargoes was difficult, particularly of coal on which the industrial development depended, for there was too little fall on the river to provide much power for mills and machinery. Coal came in on packhorse trains and carts until almost the end of the century. It came from the Swannington and Whitwick pits, in small quantities, down Coalpit Lane and then either the Narborough or the Aylestone Road, until the new canal from the Trent to Loughborough opened the way for Derbyshire coals to come in too. Even these had to come the last part of the journey from Loughborough by packhorse. Only right at the end of the century, in 1794, was the canal extended to Leicester itself and it became possible to ship coal direct from Derbyshire. The price then fell by about 40 per cent.

Leicester, then, with communications established to London and in all directions, and with the possibilities of power for industrial expansion, was in a good position to grow at the end of the century, but unfortunately growth was taking place in a form which divided the town bitterly. The government of the town was in the hands of a circle more closed than we can really appreciate. It consisted of a group of 24 aldermen and 48 common councilmen. This group was not elected. When a vacancy occurred by death or otherwise the number was filled up by the Council choosing a new member for themselves. Furthermore, all the justices of the peace, all the financial officers, the stewards of the Corporation property, and the other officers, were chosen by the Corporation from amongst their own members. With the best will in the world, and this was by no means always present, it would have been impossible for this system to operate over a period of several hundred years without it degenerating into a clique who controlled all civic patronage, determined who could be educated in the town's principal schools, who should benefit from the town charities, and so on. Its grip on the town might be regarded as firm and complete. By the middle of the century at least it had an entrenched front of Anglican-Tory shopkeepers and small producers. Against this, however, other forces began to move. Only freemen of the town might trade or have shops, and entry to the freedom was, of course, controlled by the Corporation. In 1749, after a long and fierce lawsuit, a watchmaker named Green established the right of people not freemen of the town to set up in business and to trade in Leicester. This meant that the Corporation could no longer control the town's business and industry. The old guard hung on to its retailing and trading privileges as long as it could but the new manufacturing industries grew up outside its control. Moreover, they grew up under the control of men who, excluded by the Corporation from civic power and authority, were opposed to the Corporation. After all, the Corporation controlled the freedoms, and only freemen could vote in parliamentary elections (the Corporation's self-elective system precluded local elections). On their side the new men tended to be Non-conformist. Perhaps the worst clash in the century came in December 1787. Messrs Coltman and Whetstone proposed to introduce machinery for worsted spinning into the town, and a look at a near-contemporary account brings out several interesting aspects – the lack of police, the use of a mob by the authorities, and the atmosphere of the period. "Their enterprise", it says, "was not destined at first to succeed. For not long after it became generally known that worsted was about to be spun by machinery, the workpeople, uneducated and unreflecting as they were, came to the conclusion that their labour would thereby be rendered valueless. Their feelings were also worked on by their leaders (i.e. the Corporation) to a high pitch of indignation and they were taught to look on Messrs Coltman and Whetstone as their enemies. In fact these gentlemen were openly threatened with loss of life and destruction of their property if they persisted in the prosecution of their purpose. As party spirit was then violent and bitter the populace were not slow to raise outcries against them also on account of their being well known and decided Whigs and Dissenters." The account then goes on to describe how advertise-ments appeared in the local (Tory) newspaper inviting the workmen to a meeting at either the White Lion or the Red Lion where they would be advised what steps to take "in a manner perfectly constitutional". Colt-man and Whetstone issued a conciliatory statement. All to no avail as the sequel will show. "Mr Whetstone from his being an active principal in the business and from residing on the spot where it was carried on was specially singled out as a mark of popular vengeance. He applied to the Borough Magistrates for assistance in anticipation of the menaced out-break and named the day on which it was intended it should occur, but they neglected to take any precaution or to make any preparations for its prevention." Having no help to expect from the local magistracy or from any person except his own friends and workmen, he assembled a few of the latter with his sons on the eve of the expected riot. Some of the party were armed with fowling-pieces (shotguns) and they were all stationed in the upper storey of the house, the females of the family having first been committed to the care of friends. A few hours after the precise time at which the workmen were requested to assemble at the White and Red Lions, a drunken mob gathered near the house and commenced the assault. At first they broke all the windows with volleys of cobbles. Mr Whetstone and his companions retaliated with discharges from their fire-arms, but owing to the construction of the building, the attackers were able to shelter beneath the overhanging, jettied, first floor. The mob then obtained possession of the lower storey and destroyed all the furni-ture it contained. Mr Whetstone was let down by a rope from the back window by one of his sons and escaped through the summerhouse in his garden to the ground behind his premises. After obtaining a horse from a friend he left the town in the middle of the night.

The riot had continued two hours uninterrupted by the local authorities and Mr Whetstone had been driven from his home when the mayor, Mr Dickenson, arrived on the spot accompanied by the town servants and a few constables. His Worship then said to the men in the crowd, tapping some of them on the back, "Come, my lads, give over – you've done enough – quite enough: come, give over, there's good lads, and go away." They were not disposed to take this courteous advice from the mayor. In the ensuing fracas he was struck on the head by a stone and never really recovered, dying during his year of office.

When you consider all the implications of this account and the light it throws on public order and policing as well as the biased state of the governing body, it shows how different expectations and conceptions of life were then from what they are today.

The town was split down the middle but when the century closed the industrial reforming side was still 35 years away from victory. When it came it was complete and in the first-ever elections for councillors in 1835 those who had been excluded from power so long swept the board. Not one single member of the old Corporation was returned to office.

The eighteenth century then was a germinating time for Leicester. Much of the town was rebuilt and almost repopulated. Its communications were developed and the foundations were laid for its nineteenth-century transformation into the city we still principally know and which is only now being regenerated.

Suggested reading

G. A. Chinnery, ed., *Records of the Borough of Leicester*, vol. 5, *Hall Books and Papers 1689–1835*, 1965; vol. 6, *The Chamberlains' Accounts 1689–1835*, 1967.

C. D. B. Ellis, *History in Leicester*, City of Leicester Publicity Department, 2nd edition 1969.

W. Gardiner, *Music and friends, or pleasant recollections of a dilettante*, 3 vols, 1838–53.

Mrs T. Fielding Johnson, *Glimpses of Ancient Leicester*, 1906.

A. Temple Patterson, *Radical Leicester*, 1954.

J. Thompson, *The History of Leicester in the Eighteenth Century*, 1871.

Victoria History of the County of Leicester, vol. 4, 1958.

6

The development of New Walk and the King Street area

New Walk is the sole surviving urban pedestrian way in England which links squares and open spaces of a semi-rural character. In walking its length, which is a little over a mile, the pedestrian may examine the change in style that took place in the residences of the well-to-do in Leicester from the early to the late nineteenth century; a change which demonstrates a shift from a taste firmly grounded in the classical tradition to a more strident and eclectic 'Victorianism'. He may also examine evidence of the carelessness of the twentieth century which has allowed so many of the buildings to fall into disrepair or to be unsympathetically adapted to new purposes.

The Walk, originally known as Queen's Walk, and marked as Ladies Walk on a survey of 1805, was laid out by order of the unreformed Corporation in 1785 (Map 5). Exactly when it came to be known as New Walk is not clear. It was constructed on the boundary between the parishes of St Mary and St Margaret with the then unenclosed South Fields stretching away to the west, towards the Welford Road, affording fine views. It also lay on the line of the Gartree footpath, which in turn is reputed to follow the track of the Roman 'Via Devana', so it may have been merely the proper making-up of an existing path. It was planned to be a pleasant promenade through open fields made up at the expense of the Corporation and planted with trees and shrubs provided by a public subscription of £250. It afforded pedestrian access to the race-course which was on the site of Victoria Park, but it also served to help stake out the claim of the Corporation to the rights of developing South Fields. This problem had been a matter of bitter dispute with the freemen who possessed grazing rights in the fields throughout the eighteenth century. If the fields were enclosed to suit the Corporation the grazing rights would be extinguished.

The problem was finally resolved by the Inclosure Award drawn up in 1804 and ratified in 1811 which created the Freemen's Common, between the Welford and Lutterworth roads, but gave the bulk of the fields, 453 acres, to the Corporation. To defray the costs of the inquiry ten building plots fronting the Walk, running up the east side from Welford Place, were sold by auction in 1811. The development of the area could now begin.

In fact building commenced more quickly in the newly formed surrounding streets than in the Walk for the west side was reserved exclusively for gardens and building permission on the east side was only given in 1824 with the strict provision that no vehicular access would be allowed from the Walk. The Corporation were quick to lay out new streets: King Street between 1811 and 1813, Wellington Street in 1812 and Princess Road in 1815. University Road, then called Occupation Road, was also built to allow easy expansion of estate development if the demand was sufficient (Map 5). Once the new streets were laid out the Corporation expected to sell land to developers very easily and to show large profits. These expectations were soon realized although some of the profits went into private hands as the Council sold land to its members at artificially low prices which allowed them to re-sell at market value and keep the profit. By the 1820s several buildings had been erected in King Street and Regent Road of which the most important is the Crescent, which is probably the best early nineteenth-century building in Leicester.

The first building in New Walk to which an accurate date can be attached is the old Roman Catholic chapel of 1819 which escaped the prohibition on building in the Walk by fronting Wellington Street. (It gained access to the Walk only in 1886.) It was followed after 1824 by the long terrace, today numbered 22–48, and the other houses on that side, reaching Waterloo Street by 1828. The development was not a logical progression for a gap was left opposite the museum and when the other side was developed in the 1830s the first house was No. 19 and the space left between it and King Street was not filled for about 20 years. In 1837 the present museum was built by J. Hansom, who also designed the 'Pork Pie' chapel in Belvoir Street. It was built as a private school and taken over as a museum in 1849. Demand for plots and houses in the Walk and its surrounding streets seems to have been brisk among people looking for moderately sized homes in a good social area. Contemporary observers

Map 5   Map of Leicester in 1857

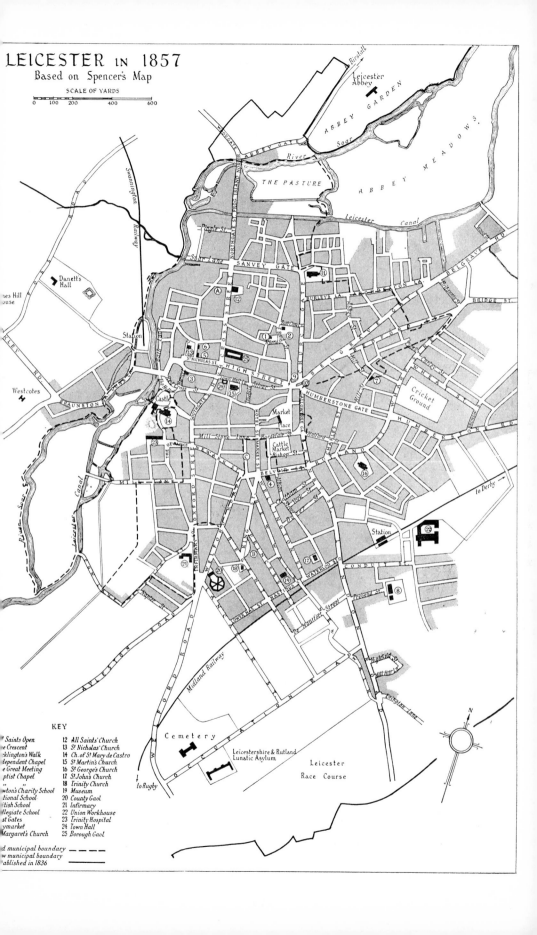

LEICESTER IN 1857
Based on Spencer's Map

SCALE OF YARDS

0   100   200   400   600

noted that a disproportionate number of the town's aristocracy lived in the area and the advertisements in the *Leicester Journal* offered plots suitable for building "genteel residences". The Census Enumerators' Books show that most of the inhabitants of the Walk lived on private incomes, owned substantial businesses or were members of the professions. They all had a servant, but seldom had very many and this, together with the size of the houses, suggests their being comfortably well-off rather than very wealthy. The houses they bought in general followed the eighteenth-century style, faced with stucco and using pilasters to articulate the façade, as can be seen in Upper King Street or Victoria Terrace in the Walk, although there were substantial residences like Waterloo House which Sir Nikolaus Pevsner, in *Buildings of Leicestershire and Rutland*, remarks as the best house in New Walk. All were tasteful, elegant and together with the trees and open spaces created a pleasant environment.

The character of this development was threatened, however, by two schemes of a quite different nature: the gaol and the railway. The Corporation agreed to sell land for the prison in 1824 without any concern for the effect its construction might have on the future development of the area. Apparently it had little effect for residential building continued close by after its completion in 1828 as in Upper King Street, the Crescent Cottages dated 1836 and the original, classical Trinity church designed by Sidney Smirke in 1838. (The church was restored into the Gothic style and renamed Holy Trinity in a period of High Church enthusiasm in the 1870s.) The railway, though, presented a more serious threat, for the Midland Railway Company intended to lay a line right across South Fields cutting New Walk, Princess Road, and Regent Road. The Corporation opposed the plans fearing a decline in land values in an area where it was the major landowner, but its opposition was unsuccessful. In 1840 the line was opened and despite a temporary drop in land values little effect was felt. The social desirability of the area was well enough established to withstand this unwelcome intrusion. Elsewhere in South Fields the railway did have the effect of ending plans to extend the New Walk development across to Welford Road, over land which was taken for the cemetery in 1849, as a gentleman's residential area. But within a few years demand for houses in the area of the Walk had picked up sufficiently to lead to the building of the terrace in Lower Hastings Street which backs directly on to the tracks.

Up to the mid-nineteenth century there is no evidence of co-ordinated planning in New Walk, a fact which seems to be typical of Leicester in this period. It was the work of many hands developing small plots without regard for other schemes. Even long terraces like Nos. 22–48 were not built at one time by one developer in spite of the outward uniformity of the design, and the individual villas differ quite widely. What unifies the whole scheme is conformity to certain well-established traditions of architecture which were the accepted canons of taste at the time. In fact, by the time many of the buildings were erected those traditions had become passé and the Walk reflects a taste that by the middle of the century had ceased to be really fashionable. It did give a style to the Walk that later developers were loath to destroy.

The most important of these developers was William Rushin who built 14 houses, Nos. 106–32, on either side of De Montfort Street between 1862 and 1865. They all presented identical façades to New Walk, though the corner properties have their main façades towards De Montfort Street and they were treated differently; one is asymmetrical, the other, the Belmont Hotel, is classical with a portico. They look like a co-ordinated development, yet they were built pair by pair, as finance became available, and to a stock design of Rushin's firm, drawn by his son, which can also be seen in Rushin Terrace in London Road. Curiously though, the villas do not seem to have been occupied as they were completed, for the 1864 directory makes no reference to any of them. They are semi-detached, three storeyed, built of red brick with details like quoins and porch mouldings of plaster. The treatment of the façade is essentially that of the eighteenth century especially in the proportions of the windows, except for the application of a bay window on ground and first floors. This bay window makes the villas unmistakably Victorian and yet they retain sufficient of the classical idiom to blend in with the earlier buildings. When they were built they represented a neat compromise between the demands of buyers for fashionable houses and the demands of the area for designs which would harmonize with the rest of the Walk. Rushin's idea of bay windows was taken up by others, including Shenton and Baker and W. Burton, and all the houses in the Walk from No. 132 to University Road are variations on Rushin's basic design using bay windows. Even more surprising was the vogue for building bays on to existing properties in the Walk. From 1872 the records show a number of owners altering their houses in this way. Their concern must have been entirely a matter of fashion for bays add little to the actual size of the room, although they may increase the appearance of spaciousness. They were added to elegant classical fronts with no regard to the violation they were doing to the original proportions of the buildings. The terrace above the Catholic church, Nos. 22–48 Victoria Terrace, Nos. 27–45 and even the charming five-house terrace opposite De Montfort Square, Nos. 96–104, all acquired a rash of varied bays. The last-named group has two different designs of bay within the space of five houses. Strangely this mania did not affect the terraces in De Montfort and Museum Squares for reasons which are not clear.

Once the classical tradition had been breached the remaining un--

developed areas were built on in a more obviously Victorian way, with no unifying architectural ideal. In Upper New Walk, in West Walk and in the gaps in New Walk much larger houses were built. Many were asymmetrical and used a violent red brick and tile finish. Gables became prominent, and replaced bay windows as the fashionable gimmick, heavily accented chimneys or even turrets were used. Most of this development came after 1880 and to see the change in taste that occurred you only have to compare Nos. 19–25, built in the 1830s, with the former Roman Catholic school, dated 1886, only a few yards away.

The other important change which begins at roughly the same time is the end of the purely residential character of the Walk. Apart from a few private schools and the Tepid Baths, demolished in the 1880s, all the properties had been private homes. In 1863 a printing works was expanded so that it gained access to New Walk, and from then on a succession of warehouses and workshops, fronting on Wellington Street, pushed up to the Walk's building line. It was an inevitable process as the development of the area between Wellington Street and London Road had been mainly commercial and its extension to the Walk was only to be expected. Again no thought was given to the effect this would have on the character of the area, for the few rejected plans were turned down on technical infringements of the sanitary regulations rather than on grounds of unsuitability.

The social structure of the Walk also began to change. The substantial businessmen tended to move out along with those on private incomes. They were replaced by shopkeepers, lodging-house keepers and professional men like dentists and teachers, who ran their businesses from their New Walk homes. The wealth of the area was probably not much affected, but its social exclusiveness was being eroded. The twentieth century accelerated these changes as the desire to live in the suburbs reduced demand for houses in the town centre and as business found it a convenient area into which to expand. The real growth of offices in the Walk comes after the First World War and ironically today it has driven the process full circle. New Walk is again a desirable area, as property values indicate, and so too are the surrounding streets. In this process New Walk has been much changed and yet it retains its charm and character, because it is a pedestrian promenade. This fact has insulated it from some, at least, of the pressures that other nineteenth-century developments have suffered. It has also enabled the Walk to survive such insensitive developments as the present 400 Club building of 1887 by Isaac Barradale and the present Roman Catholic church of 1928–58, and even to rise above the sad dereliction of the properties near the town. It was this pedestrian character and the open spaces that the Victorians prized in New Walk, and it is only right that it should be preserved today, as in the City Planning

Officer's proposals, so that it may continue to be the most delightful example of urban development in the city.

Suggested reading

Nikolaus Pevsner, *Buildings of Leicestershire and Rutland*, 1960.

Graham Potts, 'New Walk in the Nineteenth Century', *Transactions of the Leicestershire Archaeological and Historical Society*, XLIV, 1968–9, 72–87.

Holy Trinity and its Surroundings 1838–1966 (obtainable from the church).

Victoria History of the County of Leicester, vol. 4, 1958, pp. 195–9 and 383–4.

7

The expansion of Leicester in the nineteenth century

The other day I asked my 12-year-old daughter what sort of places came to mind when she thought of 'Leicester'. I was interested to find that most of the things she mentioned were of the Victorian period: the Clock Tower, of course, High Street, Granby Street, the Town Hall; then the view over the factory chimneys as you come down from Anstey; and the rows of red-brick terraced houses of Clarendon Park and the less attractive rows in the 'nut' streets – by which she meant the area of Walnut and Filbert Streets; she also thought of the parks, like Abbey Park. She did mention, too, I'm glad to say, the Guildhall and the Jewry Wall; but her observations made the point that the Leicester we see, when we have penetrated the recent suburbs, is predominantly a product of the nineteenth century – a century that turned a partly-industrialized market-town into a great centre of manufacture, a town of factory chimneys and rows of red-brick terraced houses.

The change is most readily brought home if we consider the speed with which the population grew. In 1801 the town contained about 17,000 people; 50 years later it contained 60,000; and at the end of the century 211,000. To put it another way, we can say that by 1901 Leicester had multiplied its population by 13 and acquired almost its modern dimensions.

But, of course, numbers provide only one side of the picture; people must work, and they must have somewhere to live. So, if we consider the expansion of Leicester, we must also consider industry and buildings.

Take industry first. Now it is clear that industry grew to some extent as population grew. As far as Leicester is concerned, this means that in the first half of the century the hosiery industry grew; for it was already established as the staple industry of the town. Reliable figures are hard to come by, but the number of stocking-frames in use multiplied perhaps by ten in those 50 years. But, though the industry enlarged its labour force, it did not develop sufficiently to support the growing population. After the boom that had accompanied the Napoleonic wars it experienced a long period of depression. By 1845 it was estimated that wages had declined by as much as a half over the previous 30 years. The industry was overmanned; and the result was chronic underemployment and severe bouts of unemployment, when at times a sixth and even a third of the population was on poor relief. So, these early years of expansion were hard, hungry years, times when, if you saw pallid, undernourished, and undersized men about in the streets, you at once concluded that they were framework knitters – the bulk of Leicester's labour force.

The constant flow of newcomers into Leicester from the surrounding countryside – and remember that throughout the century half the population was made up of immigrants, that is, people not born in the town – this migration to the town kept labour plentiful and cheap. In consequence the progress of the hosiery manufacture was retarded; for, in difficult trading conditions, as long as labour was cheap there was little incentive to replace it by expensive technical innovations, such as the steam engine. Therefore the methods and organization of the industry remained, right up to the middle of the century and beyond, much what they had been at the beginning of the eighteenth century.

The basis was still the stocking-frame, worked by man-power, operated within a domestic system. The typical working man was a semi-independent artisan who worked at his frame in his own home, often helped by his family. There is a passage in the memoirs of Thomas Cooper, the Chartist, relating to 1840 when he had just come to Leicester, in which he recalls that he was surprised, as he passed through the streets at night, to see "the long upper windows of the meaner houses fully lighted and to hear the loud creak of the stocking frame". The typical employer, or hosier, was not a manufacturer so much as a merchant: he conducted his business not at a factory but in a warehouse, where on Mondays he issued the yarn to the stockingers and on Saturdays received and paid for the finished articles. Only two changes of organization deserve notice. The first is that a class of middlemen appeared: they acted as intermediaries between hosier and artisan, and sometimes also managed small workshops of 20 or 30 frames. The second is that the proportion of framework knitters who owned their own frames decreased. The great majority had to rent their frames from hosiers and frame-makers – rent which would be deducted from their earnings each week. This practice, too, delayed technical progress. Frame-rent was a constant, reliable and sometimes substantial part of a hosier's income; and he was therefore reluctant to change the system which produced it. Besides, to risk his capital in expensive machinery and factories to house it would involve him in heavy overheads that might ruin him when trade was slack. Under the traditional system much of the risk could be transferred to the artisan.

We may therefore distinguish between industrial development before and after the middle of the century. After it, industry entered a more buoyant and progressive phase. There are two aspects to this: first, the technical development of the hosiery industry; second, the development of other industries.

In the development of the hosiery industry there is one landmark that we might single out – the opening, in 1865, of Corah's great new St Margaret's factory, a factory designed to exploit the new power-machine, introduced only the year before, which was the first that really enabled steam to compete satisfactorily with the hand-frame. From that point steam power and the factory began to prevail over the old traditions. By the end of the century Corah's were employing over 1,000 work-people and 95 per cent of the town's output of hosiery was being produced on power-operated machines.

During this transition to a factory system the industry experienced another transformation. It became dependent on female labour; it employed three times as many women as men.

What happened to the men whom the women displaced? They found employment in new industries; and here we have the clue to the relative prosperity that the town enjoyed after the middle of the century. Many of them took to making boots and shoes. They proved able to adapt themselves to new techniques of boot-making which traditional manufacturing centres like Northampton were slow to adopt. I am thinking of the Cricks' introduction in 1853 of a machine for riveting the sole to the upper and the Blake sole-sewing machine, introduced by Stead and Simpson five years later. The new methods proved so advantageous that by 1871 the footwear manufacture of Leicester already surpassed that of Northampton and by the end of the century it employed more labour in Leicester than the long-established hosiery industry. An important difference was that it was male labour; so that it did not rival, but complemented the hosiery industry. There was also a similarity; the footwear manufacture remained for many years on a domestic basis; it was only after 1890 that the bulk of the 'making' was performed in factories.

Another important industry grew up as a by-product of the other two. As the hosiers and boot manufacturers adopted machinery a sophisticated engineering industry developed. By 1900 it had become the third biggest employer in the town: at that time footwear was employing about 24,000 persons, hosiery 18,000 and engineering nearly 6,000.

A fourth manufacture, that of elastic-web, grew rapidly after 1850.

Although it did not live up to its promise of becoming a major industry it deserves mention because it was responsible for some substantial buildings. I have in mind especially Faire Bros.' impressive warehouse of 1898, in Rutland Street, a Renaissance palace – at least on the outside.

So much for industrial expansion – a process characterized by the relatively late adoption of the factory, except in the less important industries that I have not mentioned, such as worsted-spinning.

While this process had been going on, even in the years of depression, Leicester had outstripped all its Midland neighbours in size. In 1801 it had the same population as Coventry; by 1851 Leicester was three times its size. In 1801 the population of Leicester was less than three-fifths that of Nottingham; by 1851 the proportions had been reversed – and Northampton and Derby had been left behind. This superiority was maintained for the rest of the century, except over Nottingham; and if Nottingham surpassed Leicester after 1877 it was only because in that year its boundaries had received a very generous extension.

Why was Leicester able to increase more rapidly than its neighbours? One reason was simply that it had the necessary building land. In Coventry and Nottingham the urban area was close-packed and hemmed in by the town fields, which were not enclosed and not available for building before the middle of the century. Not so in Leicester. It is true that the urban area was still small in 1800; remember that the River Soar marked the northern and western limit of building and St Margaret's church, Spa Place (at the end of Humberstone Gate), and the Infirmary were then all on the edge of the open country. But although it was small, it was still not densely built over. More important, there was room to build beyond the existing urban limits.

Admittedly there were certain impediments; and their presence forced building into particular directions (Maps 5 and 6). To the north the Abbey grounds and St Margaret's pasture remained immune to the developer. To the west Danet's Hall and Westcotes resisted penetration beyond the river. To the south a limited expansion became possible after 1804 when the South Fields were enclosed; but it was limited because a considerable area was allotted as the Freemen's Common and most of the rest was put in the hands not of private owners but the Corporation. The sale of this land for speculative building depended to a great extent on the financial needs of the Corporation. In the first 30 or 40 years of the century their needs made possible the laying out of new streets like Waterloo Street, King Street, Regent Road as a high-class residential district of which the Crescent in King Street is the finest example; it also made it possible to provide working-class quarters in the flatter, less salubrious area between Welford Road and the river. But piecemeal sales by the Corporation could not meet the hunger for building land. The builders

Map 6   The growth of Leicester

▰ Medieval walled area and probably Roman

▰ Up to the Industrial Revolution c. 1820

▰ First industrial spread, 19th century and up to 1914

▱ Second industrial spread, 20th century up to 1939

were forced to concentrate their attention on St Margaret's parish, to the east and north-east of the town. Here the East Field had been enclosed in 1764 and put in the hands of a number of proprietors who proved ready to sell; so it was there that the close-packed terraces of red-brick houses were most rapidly extended across the green fields. The results are seen in the figures for the population of St Margaret's parish. In 1801 the parish (Knighton omitted) contained about one-third of the inhabitants of Leicester; in 1851 it contained two-thirds. As this was during a time when the population of the town as a whole was increasing at the rate of 1,000 a year, it is clear that the greater part of that increase was absorbed by St Margaret's.

Other considerations also led people to this part of the town. One was the turnpike from Loughborough to Market Harborough; another was the Loughborough Canal with its public wharf where Charles Keene College now stands. These attracted building to the segment between the canal and Granby Street with the axis of development lying along the line of Wharf Street and Rutland Street.

Very many of the squalid terraces thrown up in this period have been swept away by modern clearance schemes, as in Wharf Street. Often, all that remains are the churches that were built to serve them, sometimes after a considerable lapse of time. Indeed, one of the best ways of tracing the pattern of this early development is to mark the new churches: St George's, near Rutland Street, built in 1827 (Map 5, *16*); Holy Trinity, at the end of King Street, 1836 (Map 5, *18*); Christ Church, Wharf Street, 1839 (now demolished); St John's, near Wellington Street, 1854 (Map 5, *17*); St Andrew's, near Jarrom Street, 1862; St Matthew's, 1865; St Luke's, Humberstone Road, 1868; St Mark's, Belgrave Gate, 1872.

In the first 50 years or so of the century there was little distinction between industrial and residential quarters. Small workshops were intermingled with dwelling houses. In so far as a specialized industrial area arose, it lay along the Loughborough Canal between the Wharf and the North Bridge; and it was here that the first gas-works was established in 1821. The chief distinction was between the working-class and the better residential districts. The best of the new housing was put up in the neighbourhood of New Walk; though this did not displace the older select residential quarters in the Newarke and St Martin's, where many of the wealthy inhabitants preferred to live until the middle of the century.

In the second half of the century the pressure of population continued to increase, particularly between 1861 and 1881. In each decade 27,000 more people had to be housed; and by 1891 the total had reached 142,000. In addition space had now to be found for the factories and warehouses that the new industrial methods required. One result was the rebuilding of much of the centre of the town for commercial and industrial purposes; another was the abandonment by the well-to-do of the old select residential quarters. Manufacturers left their homes in King Street or Wellington Street for example and built factories on their sites; factories were also established in the neighbourhood of the Newarke, which lost its select residential character.

In these years the obstacles to development to the immediate north and south were reinforced. In 1877 the Corporation purchased the Abbey Meadow, from the Earl of Dysart, and St Margaret's pasture, to form them into a park. In the south the Freemen's Common retained its identity and the Corporation ceased to sell the remaining parts of the South Fields for piecemeal development but reserved them for public purposes, such as the lunatic asylum of 1835 – now of course the University – the Welford Road cemetery of 1849, the Cattle Market of 1872, the gas-works of 1877, and the former racecourse, which was converted into Victoria Park in 1882. This meant that the town continued to enjoy extensive tracts of fairly open ground close to its centre. It meant also that the greatest pressure was felt to the east and west of the town (Map 6). Building continued to advance towards Belgrave, Humberstone, and Spinney Hill; and after 1868 the lands of Highfields House provided a middle-class quarter near London Road. The most drastic development took place across the river beyond the West Bridge in the district known as Bromkinthorpe which had remained rural until 1860. In 1861 Danet's Hall fell to the builder and in 1886 Westcotes. The rows of houses began to fan out towards Fosse Road along the line of roads that radiated from the bridge. After 1880 this was the area of most intensive development.

In this period the pattern of development was affected by improved communications. I am not thinking of the railways, because, apart from the districts around Belgrave Road Station and New Humberstone, they had little direct effect on building, but rather of the tramways, both a consequence and cause of development. The first omnibus service, along London Road and Belgrave Gate, began in 1861. This did not amount to much; but the horse-drawn trams, introduced in 1874, were a great improvement; and the system was rapidly extended until the routes covered most of the chief thoroughfares. The trams were slow, and remained so until electric traction was adopted after 1900; but they gave an impetus to suburban development.

Before the trams came, suburban development had been confined chiefly to the salubrious district of Stoneygate, where a number of high-class residences had been built towards the middle of the century. After 1865 it underwent more extensive development, though still as a select suburb. Ten years later the tramway encouraged less pretentious building in Knighton parish; the district known as South Knighton emerged and the terraced houses of Francis Street, Stoneygate. In another part of the parish the Clarendon Park estate was sold up after 1875 and rapidly covered in red brick. By 1880 the parish of Knighton had lost its identity and become little more than an appendage of Leicester.

The village of Belgrave had been stimulated early in the century by its proximity to Leicester and the opening of the Loughborough Canal; but after 1874, the tramway converted it, too, into a suburb with a population that numbered 12,000 in 1901. The old village was almost suffocated in red brick. Parts of Humberstone parish had been encroached on for building as early as the 1830s; by 1880 a whole new district, called New Humberstone, had grown up. The building of the church of St Barnabas in 1886 near the railway station marked the completion of this new suburb. However, the old village of Humberstone had still escaped the builder at the end of the century. The village of Aylestone preserved its identity for some time, chiefly because it remained in the hands of the dukes of Rutland. But in 1869 they sold the manor and the builders moved in. In ten years the population multiplied by six. In 1891 a new church, St James', Aylestone Park, was opened to serve the new suburb.

The suburban growth of Leicester received official recognition in 1892 when the borough boundaries were greatly extended to include Aylestone, Knighton, Belgrave, and large portions of Humberstone and Evington parishes. This measure nearly trebled the municipal area and recognized that Leicester had now become one of the 15 greatest towns of England.

Suggested reading

A. Briggs, *Victorian Cities*, 1963.

T. Cooper, *Life of Thomas Cooper written by Himself*, 2nd edition, 1872, and forthcoming reprint.

C. D. B. Ellis, *History in Leicester*, City of Leicester Publicity Department, 2nd edition 1969.

I. C. Ellis, *Records of Nineteenth Century Leicester*, 1935.

G. H. Martin, *The Town*, 1961.

A. Temple Patterson, *Radical Leicester*, 1954.

The Victoria History of the County of Leicester, vol. 4, 1958, pp. 251–327.

8

The local government of Leicester in the nineteenth century

The expansion of Leicester was followed – inevitably, you might think – by the expansion of its local government. Reflect on the contrast between the Guildhall, the modest seat of the old town government, and the Victorian town hall, with its architectural assertion of municipal pride; think of the contrast between the mole-catcher, the town waits, and their like, who ornamented the pay-roll of the old Corporation, and the small army of clerks, accountants, surveyors, collectors and inspectors who are listed in the borough accounts of, say, 1898–9. Consider the characteristic monuments of Victorian town government – the Abbey Park, Vestry Street baths, the museum and libraries, the gas-works, Swithland Reservoir, the late sewage farm at Beaumont Leys and the unseen miles of pipes that run beneath our streets – by these you may gain some measure of what the century achieved.

This development might seem an inevitable response to the needs of a populous, industrial, urban society: but the response was not immediate or easy. Late-Victorian municipal administration was a subtle achievement, a blend of local self-government and central supervision, of amateur judgment and professional expertise, a product of cautious empiricism that took time to mature. In consequence a time-lag occurred, in which physical expansion out-ran administrative resources and the teeming centre of industry continued to be governed by the methods of a small market-town. The gap between needs and response stretched most widely just before the middle of the century, at a time when the population numbered nearly 60,000 and was increasing at the rate of 1,000 a year. The 1840s were not only bleak, hungry years for the people of Leicester, but also the most squalid years in our municipal history. Drainage and sanitation remained the responsibility of the individual parishes; it was without plan and quite inadequate. The few parish sewers were frequently choked. In so far as they operated they thoroughly contaminated the River Soar. Many streets had open ditches for drains: half had no sewers at all. The privies of the poorer houses simply drained into open cess-pits; and there were nearly 3,000 of these pits. Another necessity of public health, a water supply, was also quite inadequate. The sixteenth-century conduit, which debouched into the Market Place, still provided the only public supply. Most people had to depend on cisterns and wells; and the wells could easily be contaminated by neglected sewers, over-flowing cess-pits or even by holes dug for privies. These insanitary conditions were aggravated by the misfortune that so much of the town was low-lying. This not only made drainage difficult but subjected large areas to serious flooding, areas avoided in the past but now built over to provide working-class accommodation. These floods forced up drains and cess-pits, contaminated wells, and left behind a noxious deposit of mud. The mass of new building had been erected without control; and, though Leicester was spared the worst horrors of the age, there were enough narrow courts, back-to-back houses, and converted pigsties to menace public health. In the southern part of St Margaret's parish builders had simply filled in the many clay pits with every kind of rubbish, then built houses without waiting for it to settle and decompose. Leicester was one of the most unhealthy towns of England: its annual mortality rate of 30 in every 1,000 was exceeded by only three other great towns. The average expectation of life was said to be 25 years. That figure represents an average for all classes; for a working man it was $20\frac{1}{2}$.

This picture suggests a complete neglect of the essential requirements of a civilized urban life. How was this possible at a time when reform had already begun? For already two important changes had taken place. The Poor Law Amendment Act of 1834 affected only one department of local government but it pointed out the way that the rest would eventually follow: it submitted the poor relief of the whole borough to a single authority, the board of guardians; it recognized the principle of representation by providing for the election of the guardians by the ratepayers, and it established a central, national authority in the form of the Poor Law Commission. These arrangements survived, in the main, until 1930. The other important change was introduced by the Municipal Corporations Act of 1835. This also established the principle of representation in our local government. It replaced the old self-perpetuating Corporation by a new body elected by the resident ratepayers; at the same time, by preserving some of the old forms, such as the offices of Mayor and Alderman, it did not break too sharply with the old traditions. The new Council, which first met in January 1836, consisted of 42 councillors and 14 aldermen, representing the seven wards of the town. The number of wards and members has since increased with the size of the borough; but in principle the system then established is the system we now enjoy – though perhaps for not much longer.

This reform did much to modernize local government. It revived its authority by basing it on the new, more acceptable, principle of representation in place of ancient precedent, prescription and charter. It even enlarged its authority by eliminating the extensive liberties that had obstructed the old Corporation and by extending the municipal boundaries well beyond the urban limits (see Map 5). In introducing a measure of publicity into the Council's proceedings, its finances in particular, the Act helped to dissipate the suspicions that had clouded the last years of the old system; and an important consequence was that a responsible finance committee replaced the chamberlains and introduced a modern system of accounting.

Nevertheless the merits of this reform have been disputed. It seemed only to replace one clique by another. Whereas the old Corporation had been a Tory, Anglican monopoly, the new Corporation could be made out to be simply a Liberal, Nonconformist monopoly. For the rest of the century the Liberals dominated the Council and used their majority to maintain a monopoly of influence. Until 1876 every mayor was a Liberal; so was every important official. The first town clerk of the reformed body, Samuel Stone, earned himself later a distinguished reputation as author of the *Justices Manual*; but he earned his appointment by his zeal for the Liberal cause. The borough funds were transferred from a Tory bank to a Liberal bank; one partner in the bank, Thomas Paget, became the first mayor of the new Corporation, another became its first treasurer. Other spoils were distributed among more humble supporters. Particularly striking, at least in the first 20 years after the reform, was the influence of one small sect, the Unitarians, and one congregation, the Great Meeting. So many of the mayors were drawn from them that the Great Meeting became known as the "Mayors' Nest" and Conservative critics complained that the Council was in the pocket of a "Socinian clique".

Whatever its faults the new system was more open and more sensitive to public feeling. The practice of annual municipal elections dates from 1835. Contests were frequent and bitterly fought on political lines from the first: if the Liberals won most of them it was partly because they paid most attention to the electorate. Also the Liberals' ascendancy was not monolithic. They contained a wide range of moderate and radical opinion; and on many issues, such as church rates, Chartism, town improvements, the divisions that mattered on the Council were the divisions among the Liberals themselves. And although to the end of the century the Council's membership remained overwhelmingly middle-class the system was not entirely irresponsive to working-class opinion. The radical wing of the Liberals was strong and claimed to speak for the working man; and when changing conditions made direct working-class participation a possibility, the system proved flexible enough to accommodate it. This was achieved first by co-operation between the Trades Council and the Liberal Party, which in 1873 secured the election of Daniel Merrick – the first working man to sit on the Council. Twenty years later the Trades Council felt strong enough to run its own candidates; and in 1895 a branch of the Independent Labour Party was established in Leicester. From that time a separate Labour representation was slowly built up; and in 1909 the Liberals at last lost their absolute majority on the town council.

This survey suggests that the municipal reform of 1835 was a real reform that improved the quality of local government. The question, however, still remains: why was it not followed by some immediate improvement in the condition of the town? One answer is that the question implies a misconception of the objects of the Act of 1835. It had mainly the political purpose of ending the abuses and irresponsibility of the old system. Except in one respect it did not aim to enlarge the functions of municipal government.

The one exception was made in respect of the police. Hitherto the responsibility of maintaining a police had lain on the parishes, although the borough had in fact supplemented their efforts with a body of general constables. Now the Act placed the obligation of policing the whole borough firmly on the Council itself; and the history of our modern police begins in 1836 when the Council established a professional, uniformed force, 50 in number, organized on the model of the Metropolitan police and commanded by an officer trained in London. This soon made a marked contribution to the standards of public order in the town.

Apart from this the Act did not encourage a new conception of municipal duties. In abolishing the old Corporation it did not dissipate the old view that limited the Council's functions to managing the corporate finances and particularly the borough estates. It did not empower it to take over from the parishes the elementary tasks of drainage, sanitation, street maintenance and cleansing. It did not clearly authorize it to levy rates to finance improvements; and so, if the Council wished to undertake substantial improvements, it would have to adopt the expensive course of obtaining a private Act of Parliament.

In Leicester the new Corporation had a further excuse for inaction. It had taken over heavy debts and had to pay a large compensation to displaced officials. Its first ten years were therefore devoted to liquidating the financial legacy of the old régime. Even when the last of these debts had been paid, as they had by 1841, the policy of economy survived: the object was to finance most expenditure from the borough estates and to keep the revenue from the rates below £2,000 a year. In fairness, one must remember that the borough rate was only one of the local burdens imposed on the ratepayers: they had to pay parish rates, of which the poor-rate was especially heavy in times when the guardians were spending as much as £30,000 a year – in 1847, for example, the poor-rate in St Margaret's parish reached 2s. 7d. in the pound.

Although there are signs that the public conscience was beginning to be stirred over the conditions of life as early as 1839, and although a sanitary committee was established in 1843, the Council for long shied away from the expense of fundamental sanitary improvements. Its first efforts were directed towards cheaper and more ornamental developments. In 1838 it allotted a small part of the South Fields to form the Welford Road recreation ground and opened another near Wharf Street nine years later. In 1842 it rebuilt the West Bridge; and in 1845 obtained a private Act to build a new post office and market hall and to enlarge the cattle market. In 1848 it created the museum. Its most important achievement in this period was to establish in the same year the Welford Road cemetery – a useful contribution to the cause of public health.

However, these measures hardly relieved the miseries of the age. Effective action required the prompting of the central government, in the form of the first Public Health Act of 1848. This Act occupies as important a place in the history of our local government as the Municipal Corporations Act. It established a new department of the central government, the General Board of Health, and authorized it to create local Boards of Health with wide powers. In 1849 the terms of the Act were applied to Leicester and the Corporation now acted also as the local Board of Health. Municipal government now entered on a new and more vigorous phase of activity; in its new capacity town improvement became for the first time one of its chief functions. It appointed a Medical Officer of Health (but, until 1885, only part-time) who at once set about the obvious nuisances of pigsties, muck-heaps, defective drains and cess-pools. In 1859 it issued the first bye-law to control private building; it also regulated the construction of factories and controlled the emission of smoke. Above all it took over from the parishes the responsibility for cleansing, draining, sewerage, and water supply; and for the first time these functions came under a unified and systematic control.

The immediate result of the Act of 1848 was the first serious attempt to supply the fundamental requisites of a civilized life – an adequate supply of water and a comprehensive scheme of sewerage. In 1851 the Leicester Waterworks Company was established and a reservoir built at Thornton, from which the water was first piped to Leicester at the end of 1853. At the same time £40,000 was spent on a system of main sewers and in 1855 the first sewage works began to operate. It is characteristic of this early period of municipal enterprise that the Corporation did not undertake the direct management of these schemes. Both the water and sewage works were in the hands of private companies, in which, however, the Corporation had a large financial interest.

Although the Act of 1848 deserves to be considered as a turning point because it imposed a larger concept of municipal duties, the measures it brought about were only a beginning. Twenty more years passed before even the majority of houses enjoyed piped water; and 40 before a satisfactory sewerage system was achieved. For the scheme was defective and expensive; and a remedy had to await a new and more extravagant phase of municipal enterprise.

In the 1860s the Corporation seemed to mark time; but after 1870 it began to move forward again. This new phase was marked by a readiness to take direct responsibility for public services. Hitherto, for example, the fire-fighting services had been shared between the borough and the insurance companies: now, in 1872, a single municipal fire brigade was set up. In 1878 the Corporation bought out the Gas Company and 11 years later obtained authority to supply electricity to the town. Since 1846, in the interests of health, it had subsidized private bath establishments: in 1879 it built at Bath Lane the first municipal baths. Two others were established before the end of the century. From 1890 the Corporation had its eye on the Tramway Company; it took it over in 1901.

In these years more amenities were undertaken. The first public library was opened in 1871; five branch libraries were added by the end of the century. Together with the museum and the art gallery, adopted in 1885, these were supported by a $1\frac{1}{2}d$. rate. Parks, too, were laid out – the Abbey Park and Victoria Park in 1882, and Spinney Hill in 1886.

The most impressive achievements of the late-Victorian Corporation were in the sphere of public health. In 1878 it purchased the Water Company, embarked on expensive extensions, such as the reservoir at Swithland, and at the end of the century was planning the ambitious Derwent Valley scheme. It also tackled the old problem of flooding. The major works were carried out in the ten years after 1881. They created the Soar as we now know it, at a cost of £300,000. At the same time the defects of the sewerage system were at last rectified – though only after an embarrassing public inquiry which forced the Corporation to act. Its reluctance is understandable: the construction of new trunk sewers and culverts and the erection of a new sewage works and farm at Beaumont Leys cost £355,000 over some ten years. At a time when the rateable value of the borough was about £600,000 and a penny rate yielded about £1,600, this represented a large effort. In 1874 the municipal debt stood at £200,000: by 1894 it had reached beyond £1,000,000. This was the price of public health. It was worth the cost. By 1900 the death rate was reduced to 14.6 in every thousand.

By the end of the nineteenth century the government of Leicester had acquired many of its modern functions. Many, of course, were still lacking – the municipal provision of housing, for example, and a whole range of welfare services. Education, most expensive of all, did not become its responsibility before 1902; but the elected school board, which had been established in 1870, had worked closely with it. To perform its larger, more intricate and specialized functions, local government had to develop a professional administration. This was largely a late-Victorian achievement. Until the last quarter of the century the number of staff had remained astonishingly small. Until 1872 the town clerk had just two assistants; and he himself was only employed part-time and also ran a private practice. In 1860 the accountant had only an office boy to help him. But after 1875 a substantial municipal bureaucracy grew up. The present town hall reflects the change. Hitherto, the old Guildhall, tiny though it was, had remained the seat of municipal government. But in 1876 pressure of space made the new building necessary. Even so, by the end of the century the new town hall was bursting at the seams and staff were over-flowing to the other side of Bishop Street.

When, in 1876, the Corporation assembled for the last time in the old Guildhall before proceeding to the new town hall, it passed a resolution which ends with the words: "In closing the proceedings in this Chamber, the Council earnestly hopes that it may carry to the new Hall, that honourable zeal for the Public service which it believes had filled the breasts of those who have enjoyed the distinction of a seat in this Chamber, and when future centuries shall have rolled away, it trusts that the glory of the New Hall may exceed that of the Old." In spite of the hesitations, delays, and meannesses that at times seemed likely to betray this trust, we may nevertheless conclude that even before the nineteenth century had rolled away this expectation had been amply realized.

Suggested reading
As for 7.

9

Twentieth-century Leicester: garden suburb and council estate

I want to compare the physical development of two housing areas with the provision of social amenities in each of them and possible differences within the two communities. One area was built before the First World War, whilst the other was developed between the wars. The first area was occupied by tenant-owners; the second was predominantly made up of council tenants. Both areas were developed – mainly – outside Leicester's official boundary and both were attempts to implement ideas embodied within the term 'Garden Suburb'.

You are already aware of the growth of Leicester's population by the closing years of the nineteenth century, of the spread of housing and the extension of the town's municipal boundary (Map 6). Some people became very aware of the dangers attending a member of the working classes trying to buy his own house, and the search for various solutions to that problem and to the one of creating a better physical and social environment through different housing schemes are reviewed by both Dr Dyos and Professor Ashworth (see book list on p. 86). Garden cities were one solution and garden suburbs came as a part-solution to improving areas in an urban environment. Bedford Park in West London was such a suburb developed in the 1870s.

In order that members of the working classes could afford to live in garden suburbs we find attempts to involve workers in schemes of co-operation. Benjamin Jones, manager of a branch of the London Co-op., formed 'Tenant Co-operators Limited' in 1888. The company promoted schemes for co-partnership housing with capital from shareholders and a dividend from profits. This movement expanded and at the beginning of this century Ealing Tenants Limited was launched with its own estate at Brentham. Other co-partnership schemes were started and a federation 'Co-partnership Tenants Limited' was formed. By 1914 this contained 14 such schemes as members of the federation. One of these schemes was Anchor Tenants Limited (Leicester).

That company had taken its name from the Anchor Boot and Shoe Productive Society – a co-partnership industrial enterprise – started in 1893 and by 1900 with its own premises in Ashfordby Street, North Evington. The co-partnership shoemakers were alerted to the idea of co-partnership housing through an article, written by Henry Vivian, in the Productive Federation Year Book. In that article Vivian described the work of Ealing Tenants Limited and explained the savings in costs of house-building. In his words, "By association the tenant-owner can get everything done on wholesale terms, thus effecting a large saving."

Vivian stressed the risks confronting a worker trying to buy his own house when there was an uncertainty of employment in any one place. He recognized that one solution to such financial risks could be found in the building of houses by municipal authorities, since they could gain from the economies of wholesale dealing and offer some relief to worker tenants. Although some local authorities had entered the field of council housing by 1914 we will consider a Leicester example from between the wars. But first we need to continue the story of Anchor Tenants.

In their first year, 1902, they collected £200 as share capital and this increased to £339 in the following year. But after that the capital decreased and the venture held back until 1907 when, with extra encouragement, the share capital reached £1,500 and the company seemed ready to provide its members with houses. A search was made for a suitable site within the town boundary yet near to the Evington works, but eventually the company decided on the purchase of 17 acres, with an option on a further 31 acres, just to the east of Humberstone village (see Map 6).

A demonstration was held as the company formally took possession of the land. Vivian was there, as were the mayor and the Medical Officer of Health for Leicester, for it was Vivian who had planned the first stage development of the estate. The company tried to obtain suitable tenders from local builders, but in the end they formed their own works department to build by direct labour. George Hern was appointed manager in the May of 1908 and within two months the first memorial stone was laid by the town's Medical Officer of Health. This stone forms part of the first pair of cottages built in Keyham Lane and it offers you a chance to identify where the scheme started. The first occupants of those cottages took up residence during the October of 1908. The cost of that first pair of cottages, together with 400 yards of land for each, came to about £450 and the rent was fixed at 6s. 6d. a week.

By September 1910, 49 cottages were occupied and their gardens were well stocked as the company had made a bulk purchase of fruit trees and bushes. The first stage was completed by July 1911 (Map 7). Just as the second stage of the garden suburb was beginning in October 1911, George Hern, the company's manager, suddenly died. Recovering from the setback, the suburb increased to 95 houses by 1915. There were also three shops, an office, a meeting room and a recreation room. The population stood at 350 and the value of the estate was estimated at £33,000 with an annual revenue of just over £2,000. The business side of the suburb was managed by an elected committee of tenants, whilst another elected committee looked after the social and educational life of the community. There were regular concerts, dances, whist drives and

Map 7   Humberstone Garden Suburb: first stage – July 1911

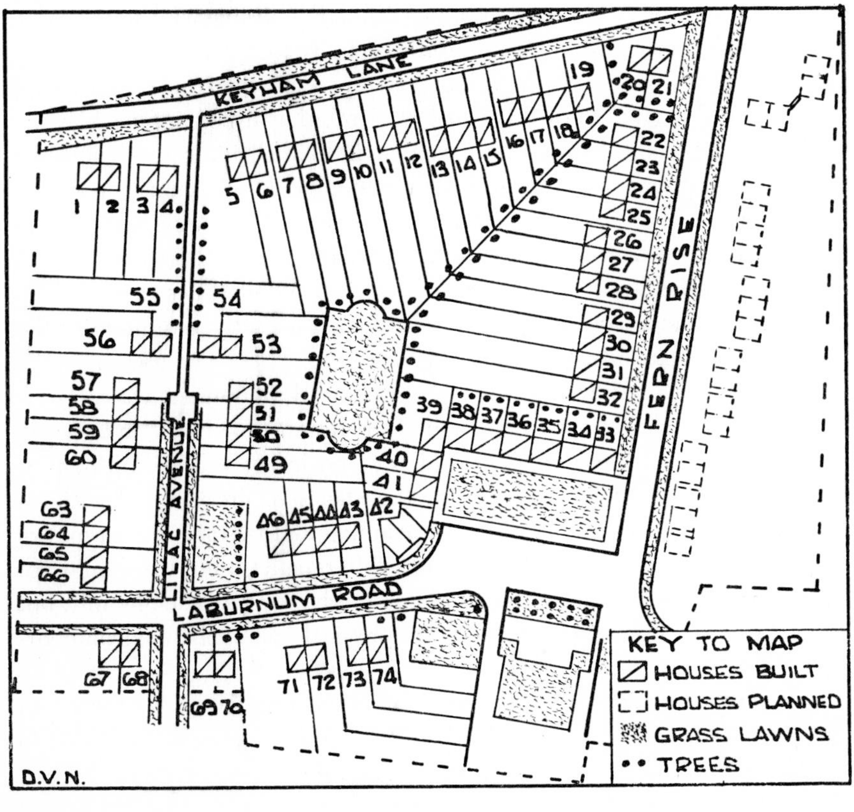

lectures. Societies and sports clubs grew in strength. Festivals and outings were regular events and the children of the suburb spent an annual summer holiday in residence at Sutton-on-Sea, away from the estate and their parents. Everyone seems to have adopted the community spirit in Humberstone Garden Suburb.

True there were certain drawbacks. Mains gas and water were available, but mains sewerage and electricity did not come to the estate until between the wars. Tenants working at the Evington factory had a journey of between four and five miles across country. All tenants had the problem of finding transport into the town, though some aid came when one tenant ran a bus service to link up with the Leicester transport service. The roads of the estate have never been made up with tarmacadam or officially adopted by the Council. The tenants have lost many of their earlier amenities. What has happened to their bowling green, tennis courts and recreational space? What was the fate of their shops and their meeting hall? You should be able to find the answers to those questions, and if you visit the suburb, a further question should arise, for you will find more than 95 houses in the suburb, showing that there must have been a third stage of growth after the First World War. When was that completed?

Before we consider the example of council housing we should pause and reflect on the community life offered by the co-partnership housing scheme and ask ourselves if Vivian was correct when he stated in his article at the beginning of this century: "Municipal housing ignores the very important and responsible part that individual interest – using the term in its best sense – plays in the management and use of house property, with educational value to the individual and the community." Did individual interest promote the community life of Humberstone Garden Suburb? Did the fact that most tenants were also colleagues at work help them with their leisure activities? Could such an active community life only blossom before the First World War?

As a contrast to Humberstone's growth and development we can now look at the four main stages of growth of the Braunstone Estate in between the wars. You will see the area on Map 6 and in more detail on Map 8. When we realize the links between the stages of growth and national legislation, which in turn influenced planning and building, the types of houses to be provided as well as the possible tenants, then we should not be tempted to look at one vast area of council housing as a single unit, but be ready to see differences in both the physical and social environments within that one area.

Our story of Braunstone Estate must start with the 1909 Act for Town Planning, as Leicester Council prepared schemes under that Act and in the Blaby Rural District referred to possible developments in areas such as Knighton, Sunnydene, Western Park, New Parks, Westcotes and

Braunstone. The next step was the adoption by the Council of the terms of the Housing (Additional Powers) Act of 1919. Grants were to be available for houses completed within one year, and the amounts ranged from £130 for a two-bedroomed house to £160 for one with four bedrooms. By March 1920 Leicester Council had accepted plans for 250 grant-aided houses, and 80 of those planned were on the Westcotes Estate, Narborough Road. The next development for housing along that road was to be for council houses and land was purchased from the Westcotes Estate Company and the Wyggeston Hospital. At that time – early 1921 – the Council had provided for 650 houses to be made available for council tenants; almost 500 of them were completed and this left only 150 to meet the then existing demand from 3,000 would-be council tenants. Further legislation in 1929 effectively halted council housing developments for a time even though the Council had already purchased land on which to site a further 1,500 houses.

But to return to the Braunstone Estate. Area 1 on Map 8 was now available for housing and the name Wyggeston Charity Estate was adopted for the proposed development of 60 houses with parlour, living-room, scullery and three bedrooms. The available land for housing in Area 1 was then extended in 1923 when the Council, having obtained an alternative site, decided to use a school site purchased in 1913 for the erection of 31 non-parlour type, three-bedroomed houses. The possibility of further council housing came through the 1923 Housing Act and under that Act a certain proportion of council-built houses were to be for sale. The 31 houses – in the Harlaxton Street area – were thus designated, so already within the first area we find different housing styles and different categories of residents.

To see the relevance of that first area it might be useful to know how much council housing there was in Leicester in 1923. Under the terms of the 1919 Act, Leicester had built 746 houses with all but 26 of them by then occupied. Through the terms of the 1923 Act, Leicester had made provision for 328 houses of which 20 were occupied and 128 being built. The demand for council housing still grew in 1924 and the Council cast their eyes further along the Narborough Road.

The next stretch of land belonged to Major Winstanley of Braunstone Hall, and he had already resisted offers from both private developers and the Council. In July 1924 the Council decided to ask the Ministry of Health for a compulsory purchase order for Winstanley's land. The two councillors responsible for moving the request were named Hallam and Gooding and their names are now commemorated on the estate. The land became available for council housing, though Braunstone Park was designated as an open space for all time, and the estate was to be planned to follow the lines of a 'Garden Suburb' development. There were to be

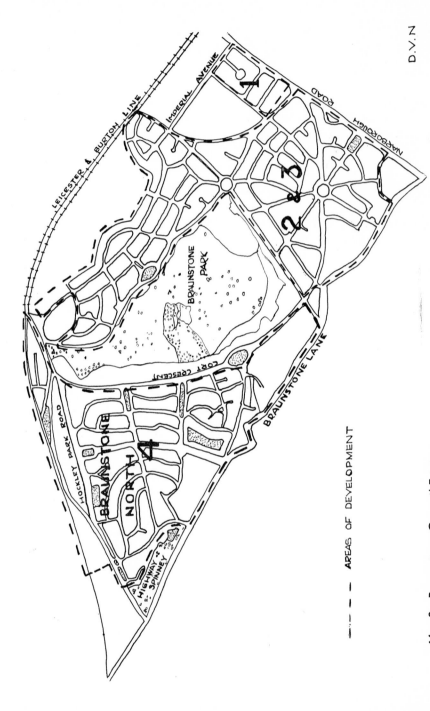

Map 8   Braunstone Council Estate

open spaces, many trees and wide grass verges. Possibly Major Winstanley influenced the use of his beloved land so that it could still provide an interesting and pleasing environment.

Mr Lanchester was the consulting architect for the estate, and the buildings were designed by Mr Fyffe; so we find that Stage 2 begins with 222 acres within the borough boundary (see Map 8). The total layout was to be for 1,200 houses and the first 500 to be erected were concrete ones diverted from the Saffron Lane Estate. By November 1930 the third stage was under way with the first 150 brick houses, and a further 341 planned for the following year. Of that total there were to be 28 houses for the elderly and these were erected off Gooding Avenue. Both Stage 2 and Stage 3, as marked on Map 8, came under the terms of the 1923 Housing Act and whereas in 1928 only 92 of the 362 houses contracted for were of the non-parlour type, by 1931 the majority of houses erected at Braunstone were non-parlour.

A further Housing Act in 1930 laid down conditions that future council housing should be mainly for slum clearance tenants. As Bowley puts it in his book *Housing and the State*, "The government had gone as near to rejecting responsibility for working class housing as it could." The terms for Stage 4 of the estate were set, but the finance was not forthcoming and the Council, already having capital invested in roads and mains services for Stage 4, did not gain any return. Councillor Harrison made an attempt to use that investment when in October 1933 he put forward a resolution to use Braunstone Stage 4 land so that private builders could erect working-class houses, in accordance with a then recent Ministry of Health circular. He was not successful and the Council still waited, though by 1935 Stage 4 became known as Braunstone North and is so named on Map 8. The Health Committee then became actively involved in the planning of Braunstone North. That committee had national pressure upon it for slum clearance and within Leicester this meant some 600 houses were designated slums with 1,850 slum tenants needing to be rehoused. Area 4 thus developed from 1936 as an area for rehousing displaced persons from slum clearance areas. A contract for 350 houses was followed by one for 274, of which 100 were one-bedroomed, non-parlour ones. In fact the records show that only 24 houses with parlours were planned for Braunstone North, and this is in contrast with the earlier stages when the parlour type predominated. In 1937 came two contracts for a further 400 houses – the majority being three-bedroomed, non-parlour types.

It is interesting to see a plea in 1937 that hot water systems be installed in the Braunstone houses, and to wonder when those houses did get their hot water systems. Different facilities for the estate came as a result of the 1936 Housing Act, for under that Act a Housing Authority could, for the first time, reserve spaces for shops or other uses and in certain cases could provide and maintain buildings. Records show that four shops became available for tenants in 1938 and that a coal yard was thought necessary. That same year three sites were sold to the Church of England and all in all this raises many questions about the amenities and the forms of social life of the residents during the growth of the area through Stages 1 to 4.

Braunstone Hall was used as a school from 1930 and Queensmead dates from 1931. What about the other schools? The British Legion opened a club in 1930, but what about the other clubs or pubs? A cinema was built in the early 'thirties but when was the area provided with a library or community centres? The answers to those questions and others that you may ask could lead you to consider and compare the provisions for social life in a pre-1914 co-partnership 'Garden Suburb' with those in a municipal council estate built between the wars. Whilst accepting that size, stages of growth and time span may have caused some of the differences, you may become aware that beyond those variables lies a further explanation, linked to what Vivian foresaw at the beginning of the century, in the different attitudes to home and community likely to develop in a tenant-owner as compared with a council tenant.

Suggested reading

W. Ashworth, *The Genesis of Modern British Town Planning*, 1954, chapters 5 and 6.

M. Bruce, *Coming of the Welfare State*, 1961, pp. 246–9.

H. J. Dyos, 'The Slum Attacked', *New Society*, 8 February 1968.

R. Frankenberg, *Communities in Britain*, 1966, chapters 7 and 8.

E. Johns, *British Townscapes*, 1965, pp. 148–54.

F. J. McCulloch, 'Social and Economic Determinants of Land Use' and H. R. Parker, 'Finance' in *Land Use in an Urban Environment*, Department of Civic Design, University of Liverpool, 1961.

G. H. Martin, *The Town*, 1961, pp. 80–3.

10

Leicester past and present

These talks have reviewed the long story of the growth of Leicester: nearly 2,000 years of it altogether, and a story that is by no means done, for the city's growth continues, taking new directions in the twentieth century as it has done so many times in the past. What kind of pattern emerges from the whole story? What sort of city is this we live in? How has it differed from others in its development?

One of the things that marks it off straight away from its neighbours and rivals in the Midlands is the very length of its continuous history. None of the other great Midland towns – neither Birmingham nor Coventry nor Derby nor Nottingham – has a history as long as Leicester's. It is true that we cannot prove that the site was continuously occupied during the years after the Romans left, in the fifth and sixth centuries A.D. But, as Mr Brown said in the first talk in this series, "continuity there must have been" (page 18), for the walls and the street plan of the Roman town went on unchanged. It is clear, too, that St Nicholas' church owes its position and to some extent its character to its proximity to the Roman Jewry Wall.

Now if you look at the great English provincial cities today – the first dozen, say, in size – you will find that only one other can make any claim of this kind. That is Manchester; and there the ground plan of the Roman town has been totally obliterated by subsequent growth, whereas here in Leicester it is still quite plainly visible, helping to determine the lines of streets we know today. As for the Jewry Wall, it is a bigger and more impressive piece of Roman masonry than you will find in any other English industrial town.

There, I think, lies one of the chief clues to an understanding of Leicester. It is a town of a *long history*, constantly adapting itself to new situations, new demands; but never as a result of violent change, which produces a complete breach with the past. There have been great changes: the withdrawal of the Romans; the building of the castle; the Reformation, bringing with it a major disruption of the town's religious and social life; the development of the hosiery manufacture from the late seventeenth century onwards. More recently, coming down towards our own time, nothing has been more important than the diversification of industry, to allow Leicester to rest its prosperity not just on the demand for hosiery but for boots and shoes, for a whole range of products of light engineering.

All this has been admirably indicated in the motto that the town has borne for the past 400 years – *Semper Eadem*, always the same. It was adopted out of compliment to Queen Elizabeth I, whose motto it was and who granted the town its charter in 1586. It has often been made fun of, as a sign that in Leicester nothing ever changes; but it has come to reflect, accidentally as it were, a deep underlying truth. I think it may be useful to weave the concluding talk in this series round this theme of *Semper Eadem*. Have things indeed been always the same, and if not how and why have they changed?

Let us look first at the relationship between the town and the country-side surrounding it. Professor Everitt, in his talk, told us what a great many markets there had been in Leicester, and he rightly pointed out that the city has a special character as a market-town today. It is one of the very few of our great towns that have kept the traditional open market-place, resisting the temptation to tidy everything away into a specially-built market hall; and the Market Place we know has been the site of markets held on Saturdays for at least 700 years. You will not find anything at all like this in Birmingham or Bristol or Manchester; Nottingham *had* something very similar, but it decided to abolish it in 1929, laying out the old market-place with genteel municipal paving and pushing the stalls them-selves into a dreary hygienic uninteresting building in a back street. You can never feel now when you go to Nottingham that you have arrived in a market town; whereas if you are in Leicester on a Wednesday or a Friday or a Saturday you are constantly made aware of it.

One reason for this is the relationship in which Leicester stands to Leicestershire. Many county towns are situated, for historical or geo-graphical reasons, away from the middle of their counties. Think of Oxford, for instance, or Cambridge or Nottingham or Derby. Leicester is as centrally placed as it could possibly be; only Shrewsbury has a similarly advantageous position. Before mechanized transport arrived, everyone living in the county was within reach of it, able to make the journey in and out again easily enough in a day, with plenty of time to buy and sell in the market in between. When the railway arrived, it became for many people easier still (though one has to remember that east Leices-tershire, with its rich dairy lands, did not get much railway communica-tion until the 1880s). After the new Cattle Market was opened in 1872, a special platform was provided by the Midland Railway to serve it, so that farmers travelling in from, say, Desford or Kirby Muxloe could get there as conveniently as possible. And though *that* world has passed, and the traffic comes in by car along the roads today, it *comes* all right, as we know very well; and you are in no doubt that the Market Place is the focus of much of it. Look at the care, too, that many of the stall-holders take to announce just where their wares come from: the names of the villages, of Rearsby or Syston, still mean something to townsmen, still seem to offer some promise of good quality in this age of branded goods and faceless multiple stores.

Here is one way in which Leicester enjoys the advantage of its central position in Leicestershire. But it is central in another sense, even more important, too: central to England itself. In the Middle Ages it owed something of its greatness – of the greatness sketched by Dr Levi Fox when he was discussing the history of Leicester Castle – to that fact, to the convenience of its situation almost on the border line between northern and southern England, practically equidistant from the eastern and the western seas. In the nineteenth century it retained and enhanced the advantages of that position, in new ways. In the coaching age it lay on a great trunk route – the road we now know as A6, from London to Manchester. Nottingham, on the other hand, lay awkwardly in between that road and the Great North Road, sweeping across the eastern fringe of its county; though that drawback was counterbalanced by its good fortune in standing close to one of the greatest natural waterways in England, the River Trent. When the railway system developed, Leicester found itself splendidly placed: at an almost equal distance from London, Manchester, and Leeds, with a through trunk route to each; and with a direct line to Birmingham to give it access to the West Country, and another to Peterborough, for the east. Whereas Nottingham – and indeed Sheffield – lay, you might almost say, on branches, with inconvenient second-class services, for goods and passengers alike.

Of course this did not necessarily bring any advantage to the town. For many travellers then Leicester became – what you often hear people speak of it as now – 'a place I've just passed through'. When mass motoring began, and Charles Street was built as an internal by-pass, nearly 40 years ago, that remark became more and more common; coupled very often with some rude jest about what a dull place it seemed to be, from those who had no idea that a town of the kind that has been described in these talks lay, still open to be seen, just behind the blocks of offices and shops they were passing. But in industrial and commercial terms Leicester's place in the system of mechanized communication was highly advantageous. Why – to take one example only – did so much of the retail distribution of boots and shoes come to be organized from Leicester, by the great firms whose names were known throughout the United Kingdom and beyond it, like Freeman Hardy & Willis and Stead & Simpson?

But when I mention those names – household words, in the literal sense of the phrase, in hundreds of thousands of homes – or the name of a great Leicester textile firm like Corah's, I think they start something else in one's mind too. They *are* great names; and yet they are not associated with any great, famous schemes of physical or intellectual improvement, with the endowment of colleges or the gift of large parks; neither are our industrialists commemorated by statues (I do not forget John Biggs. He was an industrialist, indeed; but he achieved a statue as a politician, and a politician of a particular kind. His career as an industrialist ended, I am afraid, in bankruptcy.) To put my point another way, why has Leicester produced no Jesse Boot, no dynasty of philanthropic manufacturers like the Cadburys of Birmingham, the Wills of Bristol, or the Rowntrees of York?

I think for a number of reasons. Perhaps the most important of them is that the scale of Leicester industry has always been relatively small. Though there have been plenty of rich men here, there have been scarcely any millionaires; and such fortunes as those of the great shipowners – Sir John Ellerman of Hull, for example, who left £37 million in 1933 – have never been heard of here. But then it must also be said that, with very few exceptions indeed, the men themselves have never been heard of – outside their own trade and their own town, where they have been well recognized and respected. Only one man closely connected with Leicester has ever made a world-wide name, and that is Thomas Cook, who started life as a joiner in Market Harborough, to which he added market trading in Leicester, and temperance preaching. He built up his tourist business from Leicester. Indeed he, more than any other man in Europe or America, may be said to have founded the tourist industry – one of the great industries of the world today; and so Leicester may, in a sense, be called its birthplace. Thomas Cook continued to live here all his life. He built himself a house on the London Road, and when he died in 1892 he was buried in the Welford Road cemetery. He was a truly modest man, who did not seek fame; but there is irony in the reflection that few people in Leicester today have any idea that he had anything to do with the city.

Now these characteristics can be seen all through Leicester's history. It has never produced men of national distinction. (Neither has the county. I suppose Leicestershire has thrown up only one man of really first-class importance: George Fox, the founder of the Society of Friends.) The best-known commercial man in the earlier history of the town is, it is true, remembered now chiefly for his philanthropy – William Wigston; but he runs true to type in that he is a local, not in any sense a national, figure.

So it has been all along, and so I think these talks have shown us. Leicester has seldom been in the forefront of fame or of originality of any kind. It has struck out few new lines for itself. In industry it has had no firms like Boulton & Watt, it has thrown up no inventors like Trevithick or George Stephenson; in politics it has produced no municipal reformer of the calibre of Joseph Chamberlain; there is nothing in its physical lay-out to compare with the work of Grainger and Dobson in Newcastle, or of Foulston in Plymouth. And yet it has grown to become outstandingly prosperous; and with all the faults and limitations that previous speakers in this series have pointed out, that citizens of Leicester and strangers continually draw our attention to, it has become on the whole a pleasant, a convenient and comfortable place to live in – and that, after all, is one of the things a town is for, it is one of the first tests of its success.

The theme of these talks has been *growth*; and I should like now to turn back to it again, to consider how Leicester has grown, outwards from its old centre, and is growing still. Much has been said about that by those who have spoken to you. Mr Evans has discussed what we might today call the great population explosion of the nineteenth century and its consequences in the physical growth of the town; Mr Martin has illustrated one important aspect of it in the twentieth century, in the development of a new suburb at Braunstone. Again, I think one sees Leicester following its own pattern: radiating out fairly evenly from its ancient centre, to become, as the Greater Leicester of today, a complex of nearly half a million people: yet always based on the one old centre, with none of the characteristics of a conurbation. This is not a unique pattern of growth, but it is not a common one in the second half of the twentieth century; and if you look again at those dozen largest provincial towns I have spoken of, you will find that Leicester is alone among them in this respect. Most of them already form part of conurbations – Manchester, Liverpool, Leeds, Bradford, Birmingham, Nottingham. Coventry is feeling its way in this direction – out to Bedworth, southwards towards Warwick and Kenilworth. Leicester remains self-contained. It will be a long time yet before it joins up with Loughborough, with Hinckley and Nuneaton.

Yet there are changes of balance to be discerned within Greater Leicester, and they may well be more striking in the future. The popula-tion of Leicester itself, of the city proper as it is defined by its present boundaries, is declining. (That is the general rule among towns of this kind, in this country and in many others.) But the decline is more than offset by the growth of suburban communities – Oadby, Wigston, Birstall, Thurnby, and the rest. How far will they become communities in their own right? They are moving further in that direction than could have been expected 20 or 30 years ago: with big shopping centres of their own, for instance, that must in some degree pull business away from the shops and the ancient market near the Clock Tower. But again, we can see counter-trends to this: like that which may emerge from the Corporation's policy of redeveloping the decayed areas of central Leicester for high-density housing. Here is one of the most interesting elements in the dynamics of modern Leicester life: the tug-of-war between the old city and the new outer districts that are becoming integrated with it.

All this is speculation about the future; but it arises directly from a consideration of what has happened in the past. In spite of the modern appearance that it wears at a superficial glance, Leicester is really a town in which history has played, and plays still, an exceptionally important part in determining its character. It has been through no violent revolutions, producing a complete breach with the past: in our own time it was fortunate to escape major air-raids, like those which forced Coventry, say, or Plymouth into new paths of development. There is a close-knit logic about its history, each step growing evidently out of a previous one. Its industrial history is strikingly clear in these terms, from the hand-operated frame-knitting of the seventeenth century to the plastics, rubber, and light engineering of the twentieth. Or, moving a long way further back, we can see how much of the town's development flowed from William the Conqueror's decision to establish a castle here, almost exactly 900 years ago; and how that decision, in turn, was governed essentially by the same considerations as had led the Romans to found their settlement here in the first century A.D.

There is indeed a consistency, a coherence in Leicester's historical growth to which I think you will hardly find a parallel – or if there is one, I think it will surprise you when I suggest it. Oh but surely, you may say, what about Lincoln and York and Chester, Canterbury, Winchester, Exeter? They have a history as long as Leicester's, even perhaps a little longer; and York, for example, was a city of European fame when Leicester was nothing but a little country town. Quite true, and there is the point: for none of those towns I have mentioned is a great town today, judged by the standards of the modern world. You may, if you like, think they are happier for it; and of course they all have buildings more distinguished and beautiful than any you will find in Leicester. But they have not continued to *grow*, as Leicester has; they have not kept their place among the foremost towns of the kingdom.

No, the only English town that shows a pattern of growth like Leicester's is – London: a more important place, far and away, at all times, played on by political forces, national and international, far bigger, more momentous, than those felt in any provincial town. And yet, allowing for differences of scale, similar. Perhaps I may leave you to think this one out for yourselves. Whether you do or not, I hope you have enjoyed these talks on the growth of Leicester; that they will encourage you to go and look at the evidence for the story on the ground, in the museums and the streets of the city itself.

Leicester University Press

Leicester University Press has built up a list of books concerned, though not exclusively, with some of the subjects in which the University itself has a special interest: for example, English local history, transport studies, urban history, and Victorian studies. As a result, the Press has now in its list several books concerned with Leicester and its region. Those who have enjoyed the introduction to the history of Leicester given in *The growth of Leicester* may well find some of the following titles of interest.

A Walk through Leicester   Susanna Watts

Originally published in 1804, Susanna Watts' little guide to Leicester is still surprisingly useful today, for even now it is possible to trace nearly all the features mentioned. This edition is a facsimile of the first edition, with an introduction by Jack Simmons.
$6\frac{3}{4} \times 4\frac{1}{2}$ ins   168 pp   1 map   in slip-case   SBN 7185 1073 9   £1.05   21s

Radical Leicester: A history of Leicester 1780–1850   A. Temple Patterson

A detailed study of Leicester during the critical years in which the city began to emerge as one of the major industrial centres of England.
$8\frac{1}{2} \times 5\frac{1}{2}$ ins   406 pp   1 map   SBN 7185 1003 8   £2.50   50s

Education in Leicestershire 1540–1940   Edited by Brian Simon

A collection of eight essays touching on the history of education at various periods and bringing into question some accepted views. The topics range from a discussion of town and village schools after the Reformation to the reorganization of the county's educational system in the early twentieth century.
$10\frac{1}{4} \times 7\frac{1}{4}$ ins   268 pp   35 plates   1 map   SBN 7185 1076 3   £2.87   57s 6d

*Problems of Urban Passenger Transport with special
reference to Leicester*   Clifford Sharp

Discusses the necessity of improving urban travelling conditions without
destroying our towns as places where people can live, work and enjoy
themselves, and suggests a possible remedy in making greater use of public
transport.

8×6 ins   112 pp   3 maps   paperback   SBN 7185 1074 7   £0.63   12s 6d

Records of the Borough of Leicester 1689–1835   Edited by G. A. Chinnery

Vol. V   Hall Books and Papers
9⅜×6¼ ins   600 pp   SBN 7185 1043 7   £4.20   84s
Vol. VI   The Chamberlains' Accounts
9⅜×6¼ ins   560 pp   SBN 7185 1069 0   £4.20   84s
Vol. VII   In preparation
Essential source material for the administrative history of the borough.

The Corporation of Leicester 1689–1836   R. W. Greaves

First published in 1939, this pioneer study in the investigation of municipal
politics in eighteenth-century England is now made available again. It
forms an indispensable companion to Vols. V–VII of *Records of the Borough of
Leicester*.

8½×5½ ins   160 pp   2nd edn   SBN 7185 1071 2   £2.00   40s

The Geology of the East Midlands
Edited by P. C. Sylvester-Bradley and T. D. Ford

Provides a chronological account of the geological history of the east
Midlands over the last 1,000 million years in a series of 19 chapters by
acknowledged experts. All the geological formations present in the area
are covered in a series of review chapters. An extensive bibliography is
included.

9¾×7¼ ins   420 pp   7 plates   57 figs   SBN 7185 1072 0   £4.20   84s

The Press publishes many other books on English local history including
studies of Stamford, Malvern, Cheltenham, Exeter and Camberwell.
Further information will gladly be sent, on request from Leicester
University Press, 2 University Road, Leicester LE1 7RB; telephone
Leicester 20185/22281.